ESTABLISHED
IN EDEN

BOOKS BY Carole C. Carlson

The Late Great Planet Earth (with Hal Lindsey)
Satan Is Alive and Well on Planet Earth (with Hal
 Lindsey)
Straw Houses in the Wind
In My Father's House (with Corrie ten Boom)
The Terminal Generation (with Hal Lindsey)
Established in Eden

ESTABLISHED IN EDEN

CAROLE C. CARLSON

Fleming H. Revell Company
Old Tappan, New Jersey

Library of Congress Cataloging in Publication Data

Carlson, Carole C
    Established in Eden.

    1. Family. 2. Marriage. 3. Child development. 4. Interpersonal relations. I. Title.
HQ734.C314   301.42   78-14954
ISBN 0-8007-0943-8

Contents

To those courageous and tenacious people
who prove that a family is a beautiful concept—
and to the others who wish to make it so.

Introduction

This is a book about you! You may find yourself in one of the chapters . . . or several. You should recognize some members of your family in other places.

We all go through phases. Since we are all members of a family, we each see our husband or wife, our children or parents, our brothers or sisters, going through other phases. How do we cope with our own problems and still provide support for others? Where can we find the kind of creative direction we need to function in a world gone mad? This generation is experiencing pressures and influences which didn't exist for most families twenty or thirty years ago.

A family is the natural design for living. We may become isolated individuals, but that isn't the way we were created. If the family is the plan for man, then we ought to be able to make it work. But what happens? We humans manage to mess up the best system of personal relationships God has established. We don't understand each other; we break relationships; and we sever the very life-support system which provides the energy to make life worthwhile.

A family is *unique*. It's a conglomerate of ages, personalities, and interests. With each changing phase we confront new challenges, different needs. As we experience each changing phase, we find that we assume different roles. Sometimes our role confuses us and we want to shout to someone, "Hey, understand me!" All of us need a sense of personal worth and security.

Tough times come along which jolt one or more members of a family and reactions may be different. Some find new strength and motivation—and others disintegrate. Why? What are the ingredients which contribute hope for one and despair to another? Do some families, or some individuals, have secret success principles?

We are living in a sand-castle society. Some of us try to build our homes and families upon solid foundations, only to find that we have been bulldozed by circumstances which cause the walls to cave. We're caught in the crush without knowing what hit us. In the past few years we have seen families dissolve before our eyes; one minute everyone seems to have a beautiful facade, and then comes the collapse.

This is a progressive story of the changing roles we assume within our families. I have categorized our lives as having seven phases, not because there is anything sacrosanct about seven, but the sequence seemed to develop naturally in this manner. Names and details have been camouflaged to protect identity, but the stories are real.

I am not a sociologist or psychologist, although I realize that those disciplines have provided hundreds of studies on family trends and relationships. However, there are workable, practical guidelines which provide the necessary ingredients for understanding ourselves and members of our family in all of our changing phases. These guidelines are timeless, in spite of the fact that headstrong humans—like myself and maybe you—sometimes ignore the directions.

The subject of this book is the most important topic on the world scene today. No civilization, no country can survive if the basic unit of mankind—the family which was established in Eden—fails.

I have been candid in focusing a roving spotlight upon members of my own family. Without their honesty and love I would have no right to write this story. To Keith, Karin, Rick, and my mother, I owe a million hugs for allowing themselves to be placed in some of these phases. However, for my best friend, Ward—who has been patiently beside me for more than three decades—my condolences that he is stuck with me for eternity!

CAROLE C. CARLSON

ESTABLISHED
IN EDEN

Phase I

Beginning Marriage

1

After the Wedding

*Nobody knows how to be married anymore. We have this an-
tiquated notion of what marriage is. It used to be when we said,
" 'Til death do us part," that death parted us pretty soon. That's
why marriages used to last forever . . . everybody was dead.*
                              Anthropologist MARGARET MEAD
                    Los Angeles Times, *November 23, 1977*

Let marriage be held in honor among all . . . .
                              Paul's letter to the Hebrews (13:4)

Stand up. Here she comes. Isn't she lovely? So calm and composed!
"Look at that aisle! I never thought it was so long. Please don't let me
trip. Is Dad's arm really trembling, or is it just my imagination? I'm glad he's
walking with me, I don't think I could make it by myself. I wish my heart
would stop pounding so hard. It hurts. Oh, goodness, we're almost there.
There's John. Why doesn't he smile? Smile! I've never been so scared in
my life!"
*Look at him, standing so straight and certain. He seems to have grown
since we last saw him.*
"I never thought the aisle was so long. Why is it taking so long for them
to get here? Wow, she's beautiful. She seems so calm. I wish my heart
would stop pounding so hard. My palms are sweating. What should I do
now? Smile! I've never been so scared in my life!"
As the minister begins the ceremony he asks, "Who gives this woman to
be married to this man?" Father replies loud and firm, "We do, her mother
and I," and places her shaking hand in his sweaty palm.

17

With that time-honored gesture, one support system has been symbolically transferred to another support system.

Although marriage customs vary from country to country, and ceremonies are different for various religious faiths, the marriage relationship itself has a unique beginning in the Garden of Eden. Many people believe that the Bible says the first thing God did after Creation was to establish a marriage relationship, the foundation for a family. In the Book of Beginnings, Genesis, it says that God created man in His image and at the same time He made two distinct and different types of the species and labeled one *male* and the other *female*.

According to the biblical account, God gave the first man a helper, a woman to be his wife, and said, ". . . a man shall leave his father and his mother, and shall cleave to his wife . . ." (Genesis 2:24).

This leave-cleave principle means that one relationship is severed before another is established. The word *cleave* means "to grip," "to adhere tightly to." It's her shaky hand gripping his sweaty palm. This hand-in-hand relationship may extend through all of our personal phases, from generation to generation, becoming stronger and surer with the passing years, or it may weaken and lose its hold with time and trials.

Recently a sweet little Texas grandmother was in our town for the wedding of one of her grandsons. She sat in on the bridal showers, participated in the prenuptial festivities, and watched the excited bride and groom anticipate the Big Day. She had experienced over fifty years of married life before her husband died, and watched all of the activities of her grandson and his fiancée with a rather philosophical detachment. She had experienced the struggles, the joys, the heartaches, and the fun of married life; she had been through the changes we go through as a family and had a perspective which was valuable.

She said, "If there is one thing I would tell a young couple, it would be this . . . ." I waited for some immensely profound statement, full of the wisdom of her experience, and she replied with her eyes twinkling, ". . . after the wedding, there's a marriage."

Why Marry?

What is this thing called marriage, anyhow? It's called an institution, and that has an ominous connotation. There must be some reason why two people decide to enter into this state.

"Of course, we love each other."

"I can't live without him."

"I'm lonely."

"Everybody else is getting married, and I don't want to be different."

I used to think that the first credential for a couple who wanted to get married was compatibility. "We like the same things; we have so much in common." In marriage and the family courses in college we hear that the middle children in a family of three, with similar economic, social, and religious backgrounds should have the greatest chance of a successful marriage. It was with a certain degree of assurance that I checked off those points and found them comforting, because Ward and I matched the categories.

It wasn't until later that I began to learn that, by nature, no two people are truly compatible.

The next credential which is used to determine whether the one you love is the one to marry is to discover if both are willing to communicate with each other in an effort to solve the inevitable problems which arise.

The confusion which develops over communication is with the source of arbitration. What or who decides on the authority to provide communication solutions? Who is to say who is right and who is wrong?

Many couples blunder into marriage. I know we did. We had the advantage of solid family backgrounds, but ignorance of any method of solving conflicts. The change from wedding to reality came abruptly, and then over a trivial matter.

Problem: We Really Don't Know Each Other

Shortly after we were married there was a minor crisis. It all began with ink spots. My mother had painstakingly made me a negligee from some parachute silk which my brother had brought from Japan. This was soon after World War II and everything was in short supply—especially yard goods. I was sitting on the bed in our little room in the Purdue Memorial Union while Ward finished a class. As I was writing thank-you notes for wedding presents, my pen began to leak all over the front of that lovely negligee. When Ward came back I was in tears. He thought my crying was ridiculous. I thought his solution was unreasonable. I think he said, "Dye the whole thing blue and forget about it."

I sulked and began to think immediately that the man I married was completely unsympathetic and, in spite of the years I had known him, I really didn't know him at all! I don't know what he thought; he wasn't communicating.

Women cry and men don't understand. Men find situations amusing which women think are catastrophic. From small beginnings large differences grow.

Thirty years after the ink-spot caper I talked to some young married women and wasn't the least amazed when they began, "I thought I knew him, but I didn't know him at all."

Becky was the first young wife who seemed surprised that she had misjudged her husband. She and Grant had met at a school party and began to see each other exclusively from the beginning. As their romance grew, it seemed obvious to everyone that they were a great pair. They went together for a year, saw each other almost daily during that entire time, and then were engaged for six months before they were married.

Becky said when she and Grant were going together she recognized his faults, but they didn't really make any difference. After they were married, the same faults began to bother her. She realized that she was a volatile person, easy to explode; he was calm, easygoing. She also knew she was by nature very ambitious and impatient to accomplish things quickly, but he was more phlegmatic. The basic differences began to loom.

She told me, "I went through a stage where I wondered if we were going to make it or not." Then she added, "I guess there aren't many choices. Our temperaments are very different, so we either accept each other, be miserable, or break up."

Acceptance has two faces. Before they were married, Becky was impressed by how immaculately Grant dressed. After they were married, she was bothered by the long showers he took. They were part of the same attributes, but now she was viewing them from a different perspective. Grant, on the other hand, loved Becky's drive and energy, but after they were married, the same qualities sounded like nagging.

As Becky told of her continuing struggle to accept the little things she found grating about Grant, I asked her what his greatest attributes were. She didn't have any trouble listing them: good father, sense of humor, patient, kind, a good provider. She stopped and thought about what she had said. "Well, I guess the plus factors overpower the minus, don't they?"

Another young married woman, whom we shall call Tammi, said the same thing Becky did. "I thought I knew him before we were married—we had been going together for a year—but I didn't know him at all." Tammi thought her husband was very confident, but soon realized he was insecure. He had come from a talented family and was a superachiever himself. However, when Tammi discovered how unsure he felt about himself, she realized he was not the man she thought she had married.

Where Do We Go for Answers?

As we slip and slide through the problem areas of a marriage, there are times when we need the advice and counsel of someone—anyone—who can give us solutions to some of our problems. We don't have to look very far. A well-meaning friend will say, "If I were you, I wouldn't let him get away with it!" A new self-help book hits the market and you discover you might win by intimidation or learn to look out for Number One. Almost every magazine has some suggestions about marriage and the family, written by people with impressive degrees from prestigious universities.

We had all of these sources when we were beginning our marriage. I can remember trying many marriage techniques, using the advice of everyone from Eric Fromm to the *Ladies Home Journal.* Those were the 1950s and we were in this beginning phase of our lives when we were learning to live together, learning to build a future upon what we thought was just common sense. The forces trying to destroy marriages and the family structure were not as fierce in that era. We were not bombarded with no-fault divorce, easy morality, or in-and-out-of-bed attitudes. Not that building a marriage relationship is *ever easy*—not on your life! However, if we had continued in the aimless pursuit of pleasure, without goals or direction, which we had started in those early years, I don't see how we could have survived in the atmosphere of the sliding 1960s and '70s.

By 1963 we had reached a crisis. We were confused about the increasing pollution of society's trends, and yet we were lost in the morass of the modern no-man's and no-woman's-land which surrounded us.

We plunged into political activity and the cocktail-party circuit. I joined organizations, collected for charity drives, and led a Girl Scout troop. Ward joined a prestige men's service club and brought home a fat briefcase of work every night.

There was such a gaping void in our lives, and no amount of activity seemed to fill it. There were times when I'd cry myself to sleep, and not know why I was crying. To everyone else we seemed to have everything, and yet we were so empty.

We were constantly fighting for some cause, believing that we could find some purpose in a world which seemed to have gone mad. We became standard-bearers without any certain standards for our personal lives.

Our marriage wasn't going on the rocks, it was just dragging through the doldrums. Tolerable, but dull.

2

Made in Heaven But Lived in Hell?

I think marriage is a very dangerous institution, for men who find themselves trapped, saddled with a wife and children to support; dangerous for women, who aren't financially independent and end up depending on men who can throw them out when they are 40.

SIMONE DE BEAUVOIR
The Prime of Life

Then the LORD *God said, "It is not good for the man to be alone; I will make him a helper suitable for him."*
The Book of Genesis (2:18)

Who sets the standards for marriage? Parents set the standards for their children, we've been told. For some couples, parental standards are beautiful, but others are saying, "Look at my mother and father. They're getting a divorce after twenty years of marriage." Parental standards are the grand hypocrisy of the time when they say, "Don't do as I do, do as I say."

Does society set the standards for marriage? Society's standards are "do your own thing." Look who's living together today. Since 1970 there has been an 83 percent increase in the "cohabitating although unwed" category. Recently we had a house for rent, and as we were showing people through the rooms, we discovered that three out of every four couples were unwed. There was no embarrassment about this fact from the man and woman; it was very matter-of-fact.

23

What about the standards of the church? Marriage is "ordained by God," isn't it? How many churches are educating people for marriage? How many ministers require premarital counseling, or is it just prewedding suggestions about the music and the order of the ceremony? A woman who is the bridal consultant at a large church said that after a wedding the minister said to her, "Well, I wonder how long that will last."

We've been told that the Bible gives us principles and standards for our lives. Who understands the Bible? Men quote it, use phrases for book titles and songs, but ignore the fact that God gave us these words for life's direction. I can understand why people don't understand it, because for years the Bible was as unfathomable for me as income tax instructions.

Meet the Author

We grew up in a church background. We thought we were Christians because we went to Sunday school, were involved in youth activities, and were married in a church. However, we didn't have the foggiest notion about God's plan for our lives; we sang to God in our church, prayed to Him when we wanted something, and loved Him because we were told to love Him. When we walked down that long aisle, I wasn't one of God's children and neither was Ward.

As we counted off the anniversaries and added three children to the family roster, we probably gave the impression of the solid young family. Inside we were bothered, disturbed by the unrest and turbulence of the times, and worried sick about the world our kids were going to battle.

When we began to search for answers to our inner confusion, we heard for the first time that we could have a personal relationship with a God who is really there, a God who is in command and will guide us personally. We heard it at a place we never thought we would go—a mass evangelistic crusade. Sitting in the stands with thousands of people, a simple Bible verse which we had memorized in third grade became a reality. "For God so loved the world, that he gave his only begotten Son, that whosoever believeth in him should not perish, but have everlasting life" (John 3:16 KJV).

We were changed, not by an experience, but by a Person. We accepted the fact that Jesus Christ died for us. We didn't understand how it could be, but we believed that we could have a personal relationship with God. For the first time we had the desire to learn more about Jesus, His life, and teachings. He became a reality—not just another Sunday-school myth.

How Can We Know God?

To many people God is a judge, sitting and waiting until we do something He doesn't like, and then bringing down the gavel with an ominous sentence. If God is harsh and wrathful, then why does He search for and accept all the lost, sad, and sinful people? He is a loving Father. Radio, television, mass crusades, missionaries, books, people who know Him reach out to every corner of the planet, to every home. In our time we are being saturated with the concept of being "born again" into a spiritual relationship with the God of the universe.

In California there are mountain areas which are very rugged. One summer when the children were little we went to Sequoia National Park and rented a cabin for a week. The brochure called it a cabin, but it was actually a tent on top of a wooden floor. The first night we were trying to make ourselves comfortable on army cots, easing our heads on pillows stuffed with hay. We had started to fall asleep when a crash on the porch right outside the tent flap brought us bolt upright.

"What's that?" I croaked in my bravest camping whisper.

"Just a bear knocking over the garbage can," Ward answered. "Go to sleep."

Of course, I thought, *that's easy for you to say.*

The next morning, with the grisly knowledge of a city girl that there were actually "bars in them thar woods," I started to get breakfast on a funny little stove that I had to pump when suddenly I realized that Keith, age two, was not toddling around where I could see him. I called him and when he didn't come, I began to scream for Ward. We started to search. We called and looked, soon arousing some of the nearby campers who joined us. I can't remember how long it took to find him, but any parent knows the feeling of anxiety under such circumstances. We discovered him hiding happily in the hollow of a giant redwood, amused by all the attention and fuss.

Do you think that Ward would have given up the search for Keith? How much more our heavenly Father is concerned about us! The Bible says, "The Lord is not slow about His promise, as some count slowness, but is patient toward you, not wishing for any to perish but for all to come to repentence" (2 Peter 3:9).

I'm glad God is so patient. He watched us for years, pursuing all the will-o'-the-wisps of the world and then sent Billy Graham to a football stadium to read us some Bible verses we had known but never truly heard.

It Works Both Ways

While God is searching for us, we may not realize it, but we are also searching for Him. The paths lead us into many avenues. A lovely young woman, Lorie, told me about the restlessness which began to grow in her after spending seven years in a church which preached a very positive outlook on life. She said that every problem was presented with such rosy and simplistic solutions that it all sounded phony. As her children became old enough for Sunday school, they began to complain that it was dull and that they could color pictures and make little craft objects in school the rest of the week.

Lorie and Bill began to look for something else, and one day stumbled upon a church in an enchanting park and decided to try it. They went for a few weeks, puzzled but intrigued by the teaching, until one Sunday the children complained again. This time their little girl said, "I think it's dumb to try to concentrate on an eye in the middle of my forehead." Lorie and Bill thought that sounded dumb, too, so they crossed Eastern mysticism off their list and began to search again.

"We found this church which said it was Bible-believing and thought, 'Well, we've tried everything else, let's see what the Bible is all about.' " Within a short time this couple realized that the knowledge, the truth which they had been seeking all their married life, is contained in the Bible. They are now building their personal relationship and family directions upon biblical foundations.

There are many fine families who have not used biblical guidelines and there are many Christian marriages which are abominable examples of a family of God. This doesn't alter the fact that there are specific directions given to us, and if we choose to ignore them and write our own roadmaps, we may land in a ditch, go up a blind alley, or fall off a cliff. God gave us the design.

Can a Marriage Be Made in Heaven?

If you stand on the sidewalk and watch a parade, you can see the part that's right in front of you, but not much else. We have had a vantage point from the roof of a building on the avenue where the Rose Parade passes on New Year's Day. We stand way above the crowd and see the floats which are coming, the ones directly ahead, and the ones which are past. God sees the parade of our lives in the same way, but we can only see what is going on directly in front of us.

Whether we believe God has a plan for our lives or not depends upon the concept we have of God. If God is sovereign, the supreme ruler over nature, man, and destiny, then He's not surprised by what man does. He has given us freedom of choice, but our future is known to Him. Is this a paradox?

Roger and Kay were newlyweds, and we had been listening to their story of how they met and fell in love. The series of events, coincidences, and circuitous circumstances leading to their meeting was the dream of a Hollywood script writer. We said, "It must have been God's will that you met and married." Roger was thoughtful for a moment and then said, "If God knows our ways, aren't we just pawns in His master plan, without any will or direction of our own? I want Kay to know that I chose her of my own free will."

Roger and Kay were both believers and had chosen to follow Jesus Christ willingly. However, God knows which ones will accept Him. We know that we were created with freedom of choice and are responsible for our choices; however, God knows what our choices will be. He doesn't force us, for then there would be no freedom, but it is His will that we accept Him and love Him, because He first loved us.

I believe that God places a man and a woman together, even before they know Him personally, and then will guide their lives if they respond and accept guidance. I think marriages are made in heaven, but can be lived in hell when a man or woman wants to go his or her own way.

We Met By Chance (?)

How did you meet? A couple in love enjoys answering this question and talking about all the "coincidences" of their lives.

There's a marvelous story in the Bible about two people who had a blind date and fell in love at first sight. Well, maybe it wasn't a blind date; actually it was carefully arranged when an angel guided the servant of Abraham to find a wife for Abraham's son, Isaac. The servant prayed for God's guidance and suddenly saw this gorgeous girl at the well. He knew she was the one for Isaac. Here was a marriage which was truly made in heaven.

It doesn't always happen this way. Love may be a soft and gradual thing, approaching cautiously and growing quietly. When Isaac and Rebekah met, there was no doubt that it was a divinely ordered match.

Was it a coincidence that Rebekah was gathering water at the well at the exact time Abraham's servant was thirsty? Lives directed by God are often shaped by strange circumstances which our minds could never have foreseen. I don't believe it was a coincidence that Ruth and Billy Graham met in a classroom in college. Ward and I had the same last names and were forced to have lockers and seats next to each other in high school. There was no escape!

Are We Compatible?

Liking the same sports or movies, loving to ski together or go camping, will provide a measure of compatibility for a time. What happens when life becomes a tug-of-war or when conflict comes which seems irreconcilable? Who is the arbitrator? Who sets the standards? Do you think that two people who are separated from God can have a common basis for compatibility?

If we want to establish the foundation for all of our changing phases, we need to begin at the beginning of a marriage following God's design.

If a person is a believer, he has no option: he or she must marry another believer. A man or a woman in love may rationalize by saying, "I just know he will become a believer once we're married." When the Bible says, "Do not be unequally yoked with a nonbeliever" (*see* 2 Corinthians 6:14), it means tied together when you're on a journey.

Can you imagine the chaos on a driver-training program if the student were behind the wheel of the car steering the front wheels, and the instructor had another wheel which manipulated the back wheels? Who would know where to turn? Confusion would lead to terror on the streets.

On one of the tours we have taken to Israel we met Marilyn, an airline stewardess, and her mother. Marilyn was very subdued and thoughtful during most of the trip and it wasn't until we were almost ready to go home that I found out what was troubling her. "Carole, I'm engaged to this man and he isn't a Christian. I really don't know what to do."

It's not easy sometimes to share what the Bible says. When you know that the Word of God is sharper than a two-edged sword, you also realize it has to be very cutting at times. I told Marilyn that she shouldn't marry the man and felt like a female Scrooge as she started to cry. Several weeks later, however, she called to tell me that she had broken her engagement. Not long after, she called again to say that he had become a believer and they were going together again.

The postscript to that story is anticlimactic because she didn't marry him. God in His divine plan had someone else for Marilyn.

The Wherefore-Therefore Principle

When two believers marry, they have an exciting advantage right from the beginning. They have God's standards for their relationship. The Bible is a practical book, providing us with guidelines and principles that work.

Consider the *wherefore-therefore* principle. This embodies the two most vital elements in any relationship, and particularly in a marriage: acceptance and encouragement.

God doesn't tell us that before He could love and accept us we have to change the way we keep our checkbook, the color and style of our hair, or when we eat our meals. He accepts us just as we are. The change will come as we grow in His love and seek to please Him.

Here is the *wherefore* principle from the Apostle Paul's letter to the Romans. "Now may the God who gives perseverance and encouragement grant you to be of the same mind with one another according to Christ Jesus; that with one accord you may with one voice glorify the God and Father of our Lord Jesus Christ. *Wherefore,* accept one another, just as Christ also accepted us to the glory of God" (Romans 15:5–7 *italics mine*).

Acceptance. What a wonderful concept! Most of the time we need to accept each other "in spite of" the way we are. Sometimes acceptance has to be accompanied by a sense of humor.

When we were first married and living in a trailer in a mud-filled park in Indiana, I developed a drooly red-eyed cold. I was huddled next to the heater in our four-by-six living room, wrapped in Ward's bathrobe with my hair in pin curlers and mentholated goo under my nose. A true vision of youthful loveliness. Bill, one of Ward's fraternity brothers, knocked on the door to return a book and when I appeared he said, "If my wife ever looked like that I'd leave." He thought he was kidding me, but the remark drove me deeper into despair. When Ward came home, he gave me a kiss (risking infection), and said, "Honey, you're even cute when you're sick."

He accepts me! With all my moods, mistakes, and messes, he accepts me!

Here is the *therefore* principle from the Apostle Paul's letter to the Thessalonians. "*Therefore* encourage one another, and build up one another, just as you also are doing" (1 Thessalonians 5:11 *italics mine*).

What a difference encouragement makes in all human relationships! Changes in appearance and attitude are brought about by encouragement. Business associates, teachers, people we see in our professional endeavors are not always great encouragers. Sometimes the only place we can find the encouragement we crave is at home.

Some of the outstanding men of our time have credited their wives with attitudes of acceptance and encouragement. General Douglas MacArthur said that the smartest thing he ever did was to marry Jean Marie Faircloth. "She has been my constant friend, sweetheart, and devoted supporter ever since. How she has managed to put up with my eccentricities and crotchets all these years is quite beyond my comprehension . . ." (*Reminiscences,* Douglas MacArthur).

Billy Graham has said that without the support of his wife, Ruth, and her constant encouragement, it would have been almost impossible to carry on his intensive pace.

Marriages Don't Work

We had a couple living with us for a while who had problems from the first month they were married. Every day was a crisis, and their volcanoes were always threatening to erupt. The husband said to us, "The marriage just doesn't seem to be working." Every time they had a disagreement they talked about the difficulties in "The Marriage." It wasn't long before we began to think of those two caught in a hopeless trap designed by this monster called "The Marriage."

People have to *work* at marriages. Marriage is a continuing challenge of constantly changing relationships as we experience the tests of life.

Marriage is also a seal. Song of Songs says, "Put me like a seal over your heart . . ." (Song of Songs 8:6). A seal requires heat, which may cause the seal to melt into a sticky mess or form a permanent bond. What kind of a marriage seal depends upon who sets the seal—the King, or one of His court jesters.

God can provide energy for a tolerable marriage and zest for a dull relationship. One of the main requirements is grasping some of His basic concepts.

Whether a marriage is made in heaven depends upon God. Whether it is lived in hell depends upon us.

3

The Three R's of Marriage

We live today in a high-speed technological world that knows only flux and change, and it is obvious that what served as a marriage format in the past is no longer adequate to the task.

NENA AND GEORGE O'NEILL
Open Marriage

Unless the Lord builds the house,
They labor in vain who build it . . . .

Psalms 127:1

A high-school graduate who can't spell, or who stumbles over a simple paragraph in a book, may be the result of an educational background which ignored basic concepts. Marriage is a constant learning process, where we can become illiterates if we don't learn the primary lessons.

The three *R*'s in basic marriage concepts are *roles, relationships,* and *responsibilities.* When marriage roles are understood, the next two concepts follow naturally.

Roles? Rebellion!

Why do people think they must sacrifice their self-identity when they marry? Perhaps one reason is that the idea of submission is misunderstood. Women hear this and rebel inside; men grab it and react. A young wife said, "I thought I had to give up any opinion of my own. I heard that a wife must be submissive to her husband and I thought my entire personality should be submerged in his. I asked him about everything I bought for the house—even the brands of products. When he asked me where I'd like to go to dinner I'd say, 'Oh, you pick the place, it's up to you.' I became a piece of milk toast and was just about as interesting."

What is submission all about? This is one of the most confused issues in the entire man-woman relationship, and yet the roles are clearly defined in the Bible and are psychologically and socially sound.

We had been married about twenty years before the subject ever came up. We were in the mountains for a weekend family camp sponsored by the church we had recently joined. We were very new to all of this Bible teaching, but eager to learn more. It promised to be a glorious few days. No cooking, no worrying about kids and their activities; they were occupied in another area of the campgrounds. All we had to do was enjoy ourselves. I didn't think anything could spoil this freedom from our usual fast pace.

We sat in the sun-filled chapel on Saturday morning, absorbing the smell of the pines and the comfort of being with friends. The speaker walked to the podium, took out his Bible and said, "The text for this morning is from Ephesians five." He began with verse 22 and as he read I began to feel like a nail being pounded into plywood, with one insistent blow after another. "Wives, be subject to your own husbands as to the LORD. For the husband is the head of the wife as Christ also is the head of the church, He Himself being the Savior of the body. But, as the church is subject to Christ, so also the wives ought to be to their husbands in everything."

The weekend was spoiled for me. I didn't understand the passage; I couldn't reconcile what it said with my relationship to my husband; and I began to think this whole plan of the man's role and the woman's role was an evil invention to take away my own identity. My feelings that weekend were the same as many women are expressing today in the Women's Lib movement. I can understand some of their reactions, because I didn't understand submission myself.

I discovered the first mistake is to think that submission is a one-way street, with the woman flattened out on the pavement and her husband steamrolling over her. The Bible says that the first role of a man and a woman is submission to Christ as the head of their relationship. "Submit to one another out of reverence for Christ" (see Ephesians 5:21).

As we learn more about Jesus Christ and His great love for us, we respond to that love. Is there any greater manifestation of love than His death on the cross? Our response to that love is what the Bible means by "submission."

The role Christ took for us is the role He assigned to a husband who believes in Him. Husband, do you love your wife enough to die for her?

When a man begins to complain that he isn't the head of his house, the first place he might look is at himself and how he is responding to Christ's love. It's one thing to have Christ as Savior and say, "I'm born again," and it's another thing to have Christ as the Lord of your life. This is the response He wants.

Submission does not mean that a man should be a bully. Sometimes a new believer will latch on to this theme and begin a gorillalike chest-pounding routine which says, "Look at me, the head of the family!" One man made his wife give him all the money she earned from her part-time work. Another man insisted his wife itemize and price everything she purchased at the market.

The Bible never says that a husband should be an order-barking master sergeant and that his wife should salute and fall into step with his every command.

Submit means to respond willingly to loving leadership.

What is loving leadership? In the secular business world there are companies where employees enjoy working and give a good day's work for a good day's pay. Usually the people at the top of that business or organization exert strong but considerate and thoughtful leadership. We know one company which has thousands of people throughout the world associated with it in a business capacity. All of these associates call the president of the company and the chairman of the board by their first names. They have responded to loving leadership.

Have you ever had a teacher you would do anything to please? The reason you pay more attention, work for a better grade, or do a little more on a special project is often your response to loving leadership.

I believe most women want to respond to the loving leadership of their husbands. Sometimes a woman has to be patient until he develops this quality. Many times when two people marry who are not believers, and the wife accepts Christ first, she will have to wait and encourage her husband without coming on with a heavy, overpowering superspirituality. Many men are slower to accept new spiritual dimensions in their lives, especially if they have not been taught about Christ from childhood.

We Have This Relationship

In the beginning of our Christian growth I was very impatient to have Ward be the spiritual head of our family. I wanted him to have instant maturity, to be a spiritual giant before he knew how to walk. It took me several years of personal growth and painful honesty about myself before I was willing to admit that my own self-assertiveness was hindering my husband's growth. I was willing to push, but hesitant to have him lead.

Slowly, slowly I saw Ward become closer in his own relationship to Christ as he read the Bible, went to classes, and began to develop a prayer life. One time his mother was visiting us for a few days and at breakfast she confronted me with a serious face and a concerned question. "Is Ward all right? There isn't anything seriously wrong, is there?"

"No, not a thing. Why do you ask?"

"I got up in the middle of the night and he was down on his knees praying. I was sure something was wrong."

I assured her that he often woke up in the night and prayed, and she was astounded. Was this really her son?

As I began to understand that it was my role to submit (respond) to my husband's leadership, our relationship became stronger and more exciting.

I haven't lost my identity. For years I've had a business and writing career, and yet Ward is the head of our family and I love it. I am sorry for the Women For, the Women Against, and all the other groupies who feel they have been enslaved and subservient to men. There is no slavery in the response to loving leadership. The security of knowing a woman's role and a man's role is real freedom. The Bible says, "It was for freedom that Christ set us free . . ." (Galatians 5:1).

Christianity has done more to free women than all of the religions and political movements devised by man.

One weekend I was at a women's retreat with a brilliant actress, Jeannette Clift. Jeannette is not only a fine artist, but a very competent woman in the field of writing and directing. She has been a career woman for many years and would certainly earn the respect of anyone in the Women's Lib movement for her personal accomplishments. However, when we met Jeannette's husband, it was evident that her response to his leadership was not a teeth-clenching duty but an exhilarating reality.

Many women have the right to say, "It doesn't work that way in my marriage. I have nothing to respond to except this self-centered clod who demands everything and gives little."

On the other hand, there are men who refuse leadership and prefer to have their wives make the decisions.

Principles and guidelines don't bend to circumstances any more than gravity can pull you up. Principles God gave us apply to each of us individually. *We are the only persons we can change.* We can take the principle of submission (response), for instance, and make it a part of our own life, but we cannot force it upon another. We have the personal choice of allowing God to change our attitude.

A woman may believe that in order for her husband to achieve success as head of the family, she must be behind him pushing for all she's worth. If she were beside him, encouraging constantly, the road would be easier.

There's a story about Nathaniel Hawthorne which shows the influence of an encouraging wife. He was a clerk in a government office, earning just enough to exist, when he arrived one day at work to find out he was fired. His wife said, "Now, Nathaniel, you can do what you always wanted to do." Spurred by her support, Hawthorne went on to write *The House of Seven Gables, The Scarlet Letter,* and many other fine pieces of literature which have made him one of the great classical writers of all time.

The most successful marriages are those where the proper roles of husband and wife have been established, where the relationship becomes stronger with the passing years, and where responsibilities are delegated. Now we come to the third *R.*

It's Not My Responsibility! (Oh, Yes, It Is!)

It is the husband's responsibility to be the spiritual leader in the home. When conflict comes, he can establish the communication bond again with his wife or his children by leading in prayer, both as a family and privately. The strong men of the Bible were responsible for the spiritual growth and physical safety of their families. They would all qualify for the badge of "stouthearted men."

In Genesis 18:17, 19: "And the Lord said . . . I know him [*Abraham*], that he will command his children and his household after him, and they shall keep the way of the LORD . . ." (KJV).

In Genesis 35:2: "*Jacob* said to his household . . . 'Put away the foreign gods . . .' " (*italics added*).

In Hebrews 3:5: "*Moses* was faithful in all His house . . ." (*italics added*).

A man has the responsibility for the family and it is up to him to delegate the areas of responsibility to his wife and children. Women want strong men, men who will take responsibility, who will guide and lead. Probably the greatest gift a woman could give her son would be to teach him to be a responsible man.

Does a husband fulfill all his wife's needs? Can a wife be everything to her husband? No, not if Christ is the head of the family. There are areas where a husband is inadequate; only Christ can fill the void. No woman should worship her husband or a man worship his wife to the exclusion of loving the Lord Jesus.

Yes, But What If . . . .

Does all of this talk about roles, relationships, and responsibilities sound too idealistic, too unattainable? Are you thinking, "Yes, but you don't know my husband!" Or, "What if my wife insists on taking the responsibility for everything? How can I be the head of the family?"

A marriage is like a journey. If you begin with a goal of traveling toward a Christian marriage—built upon biblical principles—you can be sure that you will encounter roadblocks, barriers, and detours. You have to choose whether the goal is worth attaining, or whether you will give up after the first few bumps.

Barriers spring from wrong attitudes. Just a few of the mental attitudes which we allow to hinder our attaining a good marriage relationship are: fear, criticism, stubbornness, and emotional judgments. You may want to add your own thoughts to this list, that's your choice. They either master us or we turn them over to the Lord to master for us. He is capable of handling our emotions, even when we are incapable. One of the most reassuring passages in the Bible is in Romans 7:9 where the apostle Paul says that he practices the things he knows are wrong and doesn't do the very things he knows he should. Do you ever feel that way? You're in good company, then, for Paul continues to say that Christ in us, the "Spirit of life" (8:2) will set us free to have our minds set on the "things of the Spirit" (8:5).

The attitude of *fear* of the other forces one marriage partner to try to protect himself. A husband may fear losing his wife and become overbearing in his attitude. Pete was a fellow whose attitude was dominated by this kind of fear. He had a beautiful wife—the kind of a girl who really swung eyes around wherever she went. He was so afraid that she might be attracted to someone else that he pulled out the submissive principle and distorted it to suit his own jealous nature. He picked out her clothes, checked on her constantly, and smothered her so completely that he destroyed the very thing he wanted most, and that was a good marriage.

Sue said, "I'm afraid of his temper. I have to watch everything I say or he might blow up."

Fear is a formidable barrier to a good marriage, and yet there is a biblical principle which says, "For God hath not given us the spirit of fear [timidity]; but of power, and of love, and of a sound mind" (2 Timothy 1:7 KJV).

A critical, judgmental, or condescending attitude is another barrier. *Criticism* is so destructive. When we criticize our mate it's always "for his own good." When *we* are criticized, however, it's usually when "I didn't deserve it." Probably more marriages have been destroyed with this tool than any other devised by man. (Where do you think the term "henpecked" originated? She picked, and picked, and picked!) Men, of course, aren't the only ones who are the recipients of this attitude. Janet told me about the conflict which came into their marriage as a result of her attention to church, Bible study, and reading Christian books. All of these sound commendable, but her husband, Steve, resented these intrusions in their relationship. He would turn off the radio when her favorite Bible teacher was on, and she responded with open resentment. Janet and I were discussing this situation and I suggested that she apply the principle in Proverbs which says, "A gentle answer turns away wrath, but a harsh word stirs up anger" (Proverbs 15:1).

The next time Steve came in the kitchen and bellowed, "Will you turn off that idiot on the radio?" Janet grabbed the Proverb and responded, "I'm sorry he bugs you," and turned it off. Steve stopped dead in his peevish attitude and sat down at the table. After a few minutes of drinking his coffee he said, "Janet, that wasn't fair of me. It's just that I hear the radio all day, every day, at work, and I get sick of it. Go ahead and listen to your program."

Janet responded (submitted) in love to her husband, and he responded to her. However, if Steve's response had not been loving, the principle of Janet's submission would still be valid.

Stubbornness is the closed-mind barrier. "I'm going to prove that I'm right." After you have proved that you are right (and maybe you are), is the result worth the effort? Winning the battle and losing the war is not very intelligent strategy, and yet we march into battle ready to prove our point with the best weapons we have. "Now you listen to me." So he listens. What else can he do?

When we allow our *emotions* to dominate rational thinking, we have become slaves to our feelings, instead of searchers of facts. A marriage is not built upon just feelings; if it were, we would all give up when we didn't feel like being married! Proverbs gives us this principle:

By wisdom a house is built,
And by understanding it is established;
And by knowledge the rooms are filled
With all precious and pleasant riches.
                                        Proverbs 24:3, 4

Returning to the "sound mind principle" in the Book of Timothy, it says, "God hath not given us the spirit of fear; but of power, of love, and of a sound mind" (KJV).

Man power or *woman* power is not enough to keep a marriage rolling. We need *God power.* One weekend while on a writing assignment, I stayed at the home of Mike and Fran, a couple who knew about God's power. Mike had been paralyzed by polio to the extent that he had no use of his legs or one arm. He was helped through a long, painful rehabilitation by Fran, who patiently assisted him in his routine living. The things we take for granted, such as dressing and eating, took Mike three times as long as a person with full use of his body. However, I loved being with them. What would seem to be insurmountable obstacles to most of us were met with the power of God in their lives.

God gives us *love* in abundance. We often hear from one marriage partner or the other, "We don't love each other anymore." Or, "I just don't love her anymore." If a couple would use the *sound mind* principle and begin to work out compromises, learn to communicate better and understand each other, love could be restored. It's the same God in heaven and on earth who gave them their first love; He can restore it again.

The barriers are there, but they can be hurdled. However, two of the biggest barriers in Phase I are yet to come. They are the challenges of bank and bedroom.

4

Money and Sex—
Gifts From God

What breaks up young marriages? Lack of sex? Lack of communication? Lack of freedom? A lack of something in the institution of marriage itself? Nonsense. It is lack of money . . . .

LESTER VELIE
"The Myth of the Vanishing Family"
Reader's Digest, *February, 1973*

A pathetic paradox of these socially "free" times is that Americans are making love more but enjoying it less.

MARCIA LASSWELL AND NORMAN LOBSENZ
"The Varieties of Intimacy"
McCall's, *June, 1976*

. . . make it your ambition to lead a quiet life and attend to your own business and work with your hands . . . .

Paul's first letter to the Thessalonians 4:11

*Let your fountain be blessed,
And rejoice in the wife of your youth.
Proverbs 5:18*

Psychologists and marriage counselors tell us that two of the areas where trouble starts in a marriage are money and sex. If God is the source of both of these elements, what is His intention for their uses?

Man didn't invent sex, although he does his best to distort it. Sex is a divinely intimate relationship which was established in Eden as a vital part of the marriage relationship.

We were in the home of a young Christian couple when the husband, Barry, introduced us to his wife by saying, "This is bone of my bones." Somehow I didn't think this was a very flattering description of this lovely girl, but she responded with a big smile, so we surmised she accepted it as a compliment.

Since God made woman from the flesh and bones of man, then this extremely personal union must be the source of His gift of sex. From the very beginning God intended man and woman to have a beautiful sexual relationship within the bounds of marriage. It is an act of marriage, not meant to be exercised outside of matrimony.

In the Book of Proverbs it is explicit that sex is for two who are married, and that this is a principle which is psychologically and emotionally sound. The success principle first gives a warning and then answers with a positive response. "Drink from your own well, my son—be faithful and true to your wife . . . . Let your manhood be a blessing; rejoice in the wife of your youth. Let her charms and tender embrace satisfy you. Let her love *alone* fill you with delight" (Proverbs 5:15, 18, 19 LB, *italics added*).

The advice is quite clear. The man is told to keep check on his natural sex drive and save it for one woman: his wife.

This is contrary to recommendations being given today by many experts in the field of marital counseling. A chaplain and director of clinical pastoral education at a Houston hospital wrote his suggestions for what he calls "Flexible Monogamy." He said that sexual exclusiveness, which has been for generations the hallmark of the institution of marriage, is being challenged today and that "alternatives to traditional monogamy are shaping up." The chaplain's suggestion is called flexible monogamy, which "is different from traditional monogamy on one main issue. The latter is an exclusive genital sexual relationship, while the former is a primary genital sexual relationship." He explains this primary relationship as "one in which two persons give to each other their first loyalty, while permitting each other the relative freedom to search for and explore other relationships, even to the point of sexual intimacy" (*Los Angeles Times*, June 23, 1974).

The chaplain has applied a new fancy label to the old recognized adultery.

This is the type of advice and example being given when biblical principles are ignored or confused. It is only within the permanent, growing relationship of two people who are married—with Christ as the head of the family—that God-designed sexual fulfillment can be experienced in the fullest.

In 1963, we were at the Billy Graham Crusade which was held in the Los Angeles Memorial Colosseum. That was the year we accepted Christ into our lives and began to experience in our marriage a love relationship which has continued to grow better each year. On the final night of the Crusade we took a couple with us whom we wanted to introduce to the Gospel message which had so recently given us spiritual birth. As we sat in the crowded stands on that warm summer evening, Billy Graham said, "No man or woman can have a truly happy and satisfying relationship without Christ as the head of the family."

Our friends were furious with that remark. "I don't see how he can make such a dogmatic statement," our friend said angrily. "We have a great marriage, and Christ certainly isn't the head of our family."

We really didn't know what to answer them then. But the years and the growing knowledge of God's principles for a marriage have substantiated what Billy Graham said, even though we didn't understand it at the time.

Sex within marriage is an art which can grow in beauty and excitement throughout the years. There are some great innovations today in Christian books on sex, and every couple who intends to be married and every married couple could benefit by reading some of these books.

Today it's more difficult to teach the proper attitude toward sexual relationships with Christian principles than it was twenty-five or thirty years ago. We were not bombarded then with all of the sexual aberrations which we encounter today. Consequently, we did not face the overreaction to sex which Christian parents are forced into expressing during the seething seventies. When the innuendos are bantered about on TV, we react with disgust. It follows that the children are then programmed into thinking that we believe all sex is dirty.

We try to check the movies for decency, and in labeling this one or that one unfit because of explicit sex, we again label sex *per se* as either pure lust or of no worth.

When God created man and woman, He created every part of their bodies for enjoyment. He created opposites so that they would attract and fit together in every way. Would a loving God equip His children for a specific activity if it weren't for their pleasure?

Sex is not the culprit in our personal or national life; it is the *misuse of*

God's principles of the sexual union. Sex is designed for marriage and for mutual response.

Today there are a lot of people writing about human behavior. There are seminars held throughout the land on how to relate to others, how to have proper marriage encounters, and various formulas for successful living. Some of them are excellent, but only when they are based on that greatest manual for human behavior ever written—the Bible.

The letters to the Corinthians spell out some sound mind principles for marriage. I love the passage which says: "Let the husband fulfill his duty to his wife, and likewise also the wife to her husband. The wife does not have authority over her own body, but the husband does; and likewise also the husband does not have authority over his own body, but the wife does" (1 Corinthians 7:3, 4).

When we are married it is our "duty" to have enjoyable sexual relations with our wife or husband. One of the definitions for duty is "respect," and that can only come through a mutual agreement.

What are some of the acts which we do out of "duty"? We learn an occupation in order to make a living. Our duty is to study for that occupation. People learn to cook in order to fulfill their duty to one another of serving meals. Most of the duties we perform are the result of study and practice.

Why not apply the same kind of study and practice to the fulfillment of the sexual duty the Bible is talking about? Christians should be the most creative people on earth: in the arts, in literature, in scientific discoveries, and in the creative use of sex.

One Christian man with a creative mind took his wife to the top of a beautiful hotel for their wedding anniversary dinner. As they were leaving the restaurant, he stopped the elevator at the seventeenth floor, took a key out of his pocket, and escorted her into a beautiful hotel room—complete with flowers and dim lights.

That's creative thinking!

A woman will respond to the tender leadership of her husband and a man will respond to the admiration and encouragement of his wife. Instead of a marital tug-of-war they will have a mutual give-and-take.

Will the Past Haunt Us?

Many couples are caught in the dilemma of how far their true confessions should take them. Should we tell each other about past affairs? How honest is honest without being cruel?

Pam said that when she got married her husband was a virgin, but she wasn't. She said they discussed it before they were married, that she told him she had confessed her affair to the Lord, and as far as her young husband was concerned, it was dropped. This, of course, shows a great deal of maturity, but both of these young marrieds were believers and knew that they wanted to establish their home on God's patterns. The Bible says to confess our sins to God and that He is faithful and just to forgive us. When confession is made to the Lord, the past is erased.

Love and forgiveness are God's gracious gifts to each of us who believes in Him. Without the knowledge of God's forgiveness we would be constantly living in a stage of guilt and frustration.

The past can haunt us only when we harbor unconfessed sin in the recesses of our hearts.

Today we see many individuals and groups that grab the concept of confession of sin but apply their own methods. In one fast-growing organization, the participants begin building what they call "honest relationships" by first confessing everything they can think about themselves and then telling someone else what they think of him. These "human potential" games are intended to raise a person's consciousness to new levels of understanding. However, if confession is not granted forgiveness, it has no justification or healing power.

Man has always taken the timeless truths of God and contorted them for his own use. I personally struggled with the concept of confession to one another that the Book of James talks about. "Therefore, confess your sins to one another, and pray for one another, so that you may be healed . . ." (5:16). I was leery of the type of confession that we see in encounter groups and group therapy, because I had seen some of the terrible hurt and anxiety caused by these methods.

However, when sins have been confessed to God, then a thorough cleansing may *sometimes* come with confession to our mate, providing we are certain of the maturity and confidence of the person whom we married.

A couple who discovered the disastrous results of confession without forgiveness were Sue and Ted. They lived together for a year before they were married, but then Sue began to long for a traditional church wedding. She admitted later this was the reason she thought it would be great to be married. Her relationship with Ted was not the predominant reason for the marriage; it was the desire for a wedding gown, the reception, and the gifts which prompted the decision.

About two years after they were married, Sue and Ted both accepted

Christ as their Savior. They started in a church which did not teach sound biblical doctrine, and soon found that they were confused and having trouble in their marriage. After counseling with the pastor they were told they were harboring guilt from their past, not only the time they lived together before they married, but also relationships both had indulged in with other partners. Without being advised on the forgiveness through Christ, the guilt grew and grew until Sue said, "What's the use. I've done so many things which God couldn't forgive!" With that attitude, Sue began another affair with someone she met at the place where she worked and soon Sue and Ted were divorced.

The past *can* haunt us. Mothers should pass on to their daughters and fathers to their sons the importance of steering clear of premarital relationships for many reasons, but one of them is because the associated guilt can sour the sweetness of a marriage.

Money . . . Money . . . Money . . . !

"All you ever think about is money!" Kathy exploded one day. Her husband pushed back his chair from the kitchen table, which was piled with bills, and snapped, "If I didn't think about money, you'd have us all messed up and the credit agencies breathing down our throats."

And so the charming scene in Credit Card Community opened. Disintegration set in after that. Money was not the source of the controversy—it was their attitude toward it. God intended us to work, earn money, and use it wisely. In Proverbs 24 we read about the fellow who was lazy and didn't use good sense. His vineyard was full of weeds and his fence was broken down. Instead of working, he was dozing in line while waiting for his welfare check.

The Bible says to work. It also tells us to know the "condition of your flocks and pay attention to your herds" (Proverbs 27:23). In other words, know the balance in your bank account and live accordingly.

What should our attitude be toward money? Some solid principles were given by John Wesley over one hundred years ago when he said, "Make all you can, save all you can, give all you can."

Today there is a reaction to the affluent society by those very people who have benefited from it. In some homes we see the young people scorning material possessions while sprawled on the all-leather couch in front of the color TV.

We had a young couple come to our home one day with the accusation that we were too concerned with making money and they felt that it was their Christian duty to admonish us. I wondered what this young couple were doing in our house at ten o'clock in the morning, when they should have been working themselves!

It wasn't long after this that we heard the same pair were seeking support for their ministry.

Our attitude toward money should be God's attitude. He is the source of our wealth; prosperity is not evil when blessed by Him. When we're young and just getting started in a job or a business, existence is usually hand-to-mouth. When we realize that it's from *His* hand to our mouth, what does it matter if we have little? The Bible says, ". . . Be strong and do not lose courage, for there is reward for your work" (2 Chronicles 15:7).

Who should work in a family? Should the wife work? At the stage we are discussing now—the beginning marrieds—it is not unusual for young wives to work. Tammi told me that she considered herself a career woman and wanted money of her own. Ten months after they were married, their little boy was born, and he wasn't a part of Tammi's plan. She was so anxious to get back to work that she resumed her career within two weeks after the baby was born.

This very efficient young woman said, "I always crowded my life with so much, but I'm beginning to see that my priorities should be as a career homemaker. My house was always a mess, I left the baby first with one sitter and then another, and he always seemed cranky and hard to handle when I got home." She quit her full-time job and began to pay more attention to her baby and home. As she continued in less-demanding part-time work, she became a calmer, happier woman.

Corrine, on the other hand, said she thought that the man should be the main support of the family and the wife's work should be for the purpose of making up a difference in their life-style. Although she was a girl with a career background, she was against working after having a baby. She found, however, outlets for her talents and energy and managed a part-time business from her home after the baby was born.

There's nothing in the Bible that says a woman shouldn't work and have a career. In fact, in Proverbs 31, it talks about the excellent wife who buys and sells real estate, and even has a dressmaking business on the side. Lydia, a businesswoman, is mentioned in the Book of Acts. She was a "seller of purple," which indicated that she had rather exclusive clothing, since purple was the color for the aristocrats and nobles.

Who handles the money in a marriage? I heard a Christian man state dogmatically that no woman should pay the bills, handle the checkbook, or even be bothered by the money that comes in and goes out. After more than thirty years of handling the family checkbook, I was pretty upset with that statement. If my husband wishes my role and responsibility to be handling the money, that's fine with me. If he wants to handle it himself, that's okay, too. But making the writing of checks a violation of the scriptural principle for a woman is ridiculous.

Two or three months after she was married, a tearful little gal came to us and said that her husband insisted it was his role as head of the family to handle the checkbook. At that point they had three checks bounce and she didn't know what was coming in or going out. She had independently been handling her own finances and knew it was a skill she had. When her husband realized that a wise head delegates responsibilities, he asked his wife to take over the checkbook and peace was restored.

Today there are many people making absolute statements on the role of the man and the role of the woman which transcend common sense. Submitting to one another is a principle of mutual respect and that means working as a team, doing the things that we do the best. One Saturday afternoon Ward made a gate for the driveway while I put together a casserole for a potluck. I'm not good at carpentry and he's no better at cooking. Fortunately, God seems to have instilled certain basic abilities into men and women which are different. If Ward had wanted to cook and I had the great desire and talent to build, I do not see that we would be twisting our marriage roles.

Second money principle is to save it. If everyone wrote a check to their Christian account and a check to their savings account before the other bills, their finances would be easier to handle. An amount of our income, which is not indicated explicitly in the Scriptures, should be put in a separate account. From that account all checks should be written for the purposes God lays upon our hearts. Then, when a need is brought to our attention, we are able to go to that storehouse of God's riches and reach in to supply the need.

Credit, if used wisely and paid back regularly and promptly, is a necessary part of the society we live in. However, believers should not disgrace the Lord's name by contracting debts they cannot pay, neither should a believer borrow money he knows he cannot pay back.

Third principle of money is give all you can.

My dad told me never to lend money to a friend, that I would lose the money and lose the friend. "If the friend needs money, give it to him," he said, "with no strings attached."

One of the most difficult things about giving is to give without bragging. The story is told about a group of people attending a large fund-raising dinner. As the fervor of the evening reached a pitch, one man, anxious to start the pledges rolling in for their cause, stood up and shouted, "I wish to give a thousand dollars anonymously!"

Jesus said when you give, do not let your left hand know what your right hand is doing. Give in secret and God, who sees in secret (and He sees the intent of our hearts), will repay us in secret.

We were in a church once where we were "challenged" to pledge a certain amount and then all the pledges were posted. That wasn't a challenge—that was blackmail! God doesn't blackmail us into giving; He blesses us into extending ourselves.

With all of the books and articles bombarding us on the subjects of sex and money, it seems to me that the logical action is to go to the Source Book. It makes sense.

Phase I of beginning marriage has a predominant concern which hasn't been considered. However, it is a subject which is always present, either dominantly or subliminally. It's the contemplation of another life in the one-plus-one relationship. Should we or shouldn't we? When or never?

Phase II

Planned or Unplanned Parenthood

5

Wanted or Accident?

The 44,350,000 potential mothers in our country have become the target of an immense amount of propaganda urging them not to have children.

SAMUEL BLUMENFELD
The Retreat from Motherhood

Behold, children are a gift of the LORD;
The fruit of the womb is a reward.
Psalms 127:3

The two couples were studies in contrast, but they both said the same thing. "We don't want children." The first couple said with unabashed frankness, "Kids are okay . . . as long as they belong to someone else. We don't want to be tied down. We love to ski, go out to dinner, have nice cars, and a baby would stop a lot of that."

The second view was expressed by the other pair who said, "We don't think it's fair to bring a child into a world like this. The population crisis makes it morally unfeasible."

One selfish view, one idealistic approach. Both views are the result of the antibaby advocates who are pushing parenthood into an extinct state.

In his book *The Population Bomb,* Paul Ehrlich gave fuel to the alarmists who took his frightening specter of overpopulation and have exerted an enormous influence on the thinking patterns of young people. The anti-population protagonists have pushed the panic button in so many places that many fine couples are saying it is their duty to mankind to remain childless.

The couples who say that children would inhibit their life-style have some firm advocates for this view in a group called "National Organization for Non Parents." NON held a West Coast convention in 1976 and said that the most important decision you will ever have to make is whether or not to have a baby. When the membership was surveyed for reasons for their antibaby outlook, it was reported that "their main reason for not having children was that child rearing reduces the ability to do what one wants when one wants. A secondary reason was that it intrudes on one's relationship with a spouse" (*Los Angeles Times,* Part IV, May 26, 1976).

What Is an Inhibited Life-style?

I'm not sure that I can offer to those couples who see children as a frightful hindrance any arguments to change their opinion. All we can do is show a richer alternative which they may never experience, if they remain childless.

Anything worth having has a cost, and a baby costs the mother something, first of all. Our first child was born four years after we were married. She was wanted so intensely that when we finally knew the certainty of my pregnancy, we wanted to issue an all-points bulletin! Everyone who has a first baby thinks they are the most unusual people in the world.

My doctor was young and trained in the most modern methods of obstetrics, so when we told him that I wanted to follow the Dr. Grantly Dick Read method of natural childbirth, he wasn't very enthused. However, he agreed to indulge this strange desire of mine and encouraged me through all of the exercises, breathing, and relaxation.

In our society today the trend toward natural childbirth is returning. The most important aspect of this decision is the complete cooperation of the doctor and utter confidence in his instructions. Our second child was born without the cooperation of the doctor in the final stages; he gave me sodium pentothal without my realizing it. I shall never forget the contrast between the joy and exhilaration of natural childbirth and the disappointing, fog-filled mental attitude of birth under anesthesia.

However, whether with natural childbirth, Caesarean, or anesthetized, having a baby is an exquisite gift from God. It is cooperating with God in bringing life into the world.

Every woman who has had a baby knows varying degrees of pain and discomfort, but most of them will agree that this verse in the Bible is true: "Whenever a woman is in travail she has sorrow, because her hour has come; but when she gives birth to the child, she remembers the anguish no more, for joy that a child has been born into the world" (John 16:21).

A child adds dimension to every aspect of life. A child makes love a consuming reality. A child makes personal sacrifice a willing endeavor. A child makes work a purposeful challenge.

Our daughter brought little Erin, our granddaughter, to our house, and as we watched her run down the hall in hot pursuit of our elusive cat, Karin said, "I love her so much it hurts." There's probably not a mother or a father who hasn't said or thought that at some time.

Parenthood should be a status symbol. I'm out to wave the flag in defiance of those who have called the retreat.

Vices of the VCs

One of the popular terms for young marrieds is to be VCs, which means *voluntarily childless.* They are promoting the idea that children are a liability, both economically and socially, and that a couple can have that smashing life-style they desire without being hampered by the diaper bag.

There is no answer for those who say that children are a money drain. It's true. This is a trend which has accelerated within the past two generations. Fifty or more years ago children used to be an economic asset. There were more hands to work on the farm, more help in the shop, or more cooperation with the chores at home. Today, with skyrocketing inflation, the cost of having a baby and raising a child follows the same curve as the national debt.

However, having a baby can be very motivating. A young father begins to see that he has a valid reason for being responsible on his job, for achieving success in his work. A person can say that he has certain goals in life, but without the reasons for striving toward those goals, they become empty desires. I know a young man in Canada who brought his wife and first baby home and didn't have enough money for the medicine the doctor prescribed for the baby. Jim had been given a chance to start a little business of his own after his hours teaching school, and had turned it down because he didn't have the motivating reasons to work harder. Now he had them. He started that little part-time business and within a few years built it into one of the largest business organizations of its kind in Canada. Yes, babies are very motivating.

What Happened to the "Baby Boom"?

In one generation the scale has been tipped from the baby boom to the voluntarily childless. Is the law of economic liability the main reason? Let's see what began to happen to make the baby boom a bust.

After World War II, along with the well-publicized increase in our population, there was a term born which was called "togetherness." This idea was promoted by one of our national women's magazines and it extended to everything from matching clothes to the security of returning to basic family values. The war had uprooted families, and when it was over, the desire was for a home safe from the tense, evil times of a global world war.

Just a decade later, "togetherness" began to fall apart. In the 1960s the Playboy philosophy was promoted by the bunnies and perpetuated by the rabbits. A society cannot be run by rabbits. The stability of male self-discipline was replaced by the hedonistic style of "swing, be free, live it up."

American women reacted to the Playboy philosophy in their own search for liberation. I believe most women in America thought they had already been emancipated before the feminist movement began to tell us we were all enslaved. One of the women's libber clichés seems to be that the only place a man and a woman have equality is in the voting booth. Nonsense. We are equal in God's eyes. When we accept Christ as our Savior, we are one in Christ. There is no one more liberated than a Christian woman!

There are so many things that women do better than men—and that men do better than women—that I've never understood all the fuss about equal rights. Why don't we play to our strengths? If a woman has a consuming desire to be a fireperson or handle a jackhammer on a construction crew, then give her a chance to try. However, I've never met the man who could have a baby. I don't believe many women have the physical strength to manuever a piece of earth-moving machinery, and I'm not so sure many men would have the physical stamina to experience childbirth. (The last statement can never be proven, so just pass it off as personal opinion!)

The voices of the feminists began to be stronger and more strident, which tended to undermine the strength of the men. What began to suffer?

The family. Togetherness began to capitulate to separation.

What has happened since the women's magazines of the fifties promoted togetherness? They used to feature pictures of attractive children, or mothers with babies snuggling against their breasts. Now we see breasts without the babies. As the reasons for having children and establishing permanent families began to crumble, the arguments of the voluntarily childless became stronger.

However, the standards that God has designed are different.

God Gives the Reasons for Children

The central factor in having children and establishing a family is the simple knowledge that God ordained the family and that children are His gifts. The Psalmist says:

> Unless the LORD builds the house,
> They labor in vain who build it . . . .
> Behold, children are a gift of the LORD;
> The fruit of the womb is a reward.
> Like arrows in the hand of a warrior,
> So are the children of one's youth.
> How blessed is the man whose quiver is full of them.
> Psalms 127:1, 3–5

If God established the institution of the family and children are His gifts, why are people so confused about the issue of parenthood today? At the same time that people are being urged to have fewer children, they are encouraged to have more sex. Consequently, the easy contraceptive information and the abortion mills are proliferating on the scene. It is not my intention to take up birth control methods in this book, except to say that I find no biblical guidelines to tell me that birth control within a marriage is wrong. Every couple anticipating marriage should discuss this important subject with a doctor or qualified counselor so that there is no misunderstanding about this aspect of their relationship.

Are They Worth All the Trouble?

Having children is a responsibility—a big responsibility. Is a couple willing to assume that responsibility? Many people aren't, after they see the problems children present. In a major story on families in *Newsweek*, March 12, 1973, the alarming trend toward desire to escape parental responsibility was reported: "Many people seem to need relief from parenting. One of the more startling developments in recent years is the growing number of broken families in which neither parent wants custody."

However, millions of people can tell you, "Having a baby and watching him grow is one of the most fulfilling experiences a human being can have."

An old Jewish saying is: "Not to beget children is to impair the divine image."

A child interrupts sleep, challenges stamina, and threatens the finances. But a child wraps his fist around your finger and focuses your heart on the importance of life.

God-Planned Parenthood

A good friend was telling me about the lasting impression which the story about her birth day made upon her. Two older sisters had preceded her in the family, followed by a brother who had died in childbirth. When she was born, her father walked into the room, took one look at her and said, "Another girl, humph . . ." and walked out. She later became very close to her father, but it took her years to get over the feeling of rejection in not being the sex he wanted.

It's usually not intended to hurt, but sometimes parents tell their child he was an accident. We know that accidents just happen, and that planned events are intentional. Wouldn't anyone prefer to believe he was planned?

God does have a plan for His children. When He gives a couple a child, it is a carefully planned gift.

When Karin was pregnant with her first baby, a very dear and wonderful woman was having dinner with us. She is the beloved Dutch woman, Corrie ten Boom, who wrote the inspiring book *The Hiding Place,* among others. Corrie said in her thick Dutch accent, "I should like to pray for your baby." She put her hand on Karin and felt the baby stirring. Her prayer was, "Dear Lord, we know that You see and know all about this dear little one. Protect him while he grows in the warmth of his mother's womb. When it is time for him to leave his hiding place, wrap him in Your loving arms and bring him safely into this world. Hallelujah! *Amen."*

Corrie prayed for him who turned out to be her, but I believe one of the most tender moments I've ever experienced was the night Corrie ten Boom prayed for our unborn grandchild.

Many mentally, physically, and spiritually creative people are being deceived into believing that parenthood is not an exciting outlet for their talents.

God is the chief executive of the organization of Planned Parenthood, and He knows the members of His family before they join the world.

You mean to say that God really knows us before we are born? If that is true, then there's another major issue on the national scene today—stronger than the voices of nonparenthood—but having some philosophical agreements with those views.

What if a baby is not only *unplanned,* but also utterly *unwanted* and *undesirable?* Is it fair to bring a child like that into the world?

6

Made in Secret

Vital statistics among the citizens in the nation's capital include a record of more legal abortions than live births, according to the Department of Human Resources . . . For 1976: 12,945 legal abortions compared with 9,634 live births.

PRESBYTERIAN JOURNAL
September 14, 1977

Many right-to-lifers oppose abortion not only on religious and philosophical grounds but also out of fear that it will contribute to the breakdown of the American family and further erode moral standards.

TIME *MAGAZINE*
December 19, 1977

Dianne flopped down at the kitchen table, angry at what she believe was an unjust question. I poured her a cup of coffee and she told me about calling an obstetrician for an appointment to see if she were pregnant and being asked, "Is this a wanted pregnancy?"

"That really made me mad. We have been married for four years, we have been praying for a baby, and then I'm asked an insulting question like that!"

What Dianne felt was an unjust question was simply a reflection of our times. An Ob is confronted constantly with women who seek to terminate the life which is growing within them. He has to know before he accepts them as patients.

How important is life? When does life begin? In the past few years a revolution has swept through America which has changed the attitude of many non-Christians and confused the standards of many Christians. That revolution has been in both the legislation and practice of abortion in America. Until 1967, only a few states permitted abortions, and then only if the physical health of the mother was at stake. Until that time, most of the abortions performed in the United States were illegal.

However, then the laws began to change rapidly. In 1973, the Supreme Court really opened the way to "abortion on demand" by declaring anti-abortion laws unconstitutional.

The Court seemed to base the abortion decision on the right of privacy, reasoning that a woman has a right to decide what to do with her own body. It's curious that fathers are scarcely considered in the lengthy majority opinion of the court.

Edith Schaeffer, the wife of the prominent theologian, Francis Schaeffer, tells about her childhood in China when she learned that unwanted girl babies were thrown into a pagoda and left to die on the heap of bones of all other unwanted girl babies. She said, "I remember my fierce fury that babies could be thrown away by mothers who had had them growing inside them. I remember the baby wrapped in a piece of paper and left on the doorstep of our compound, to be cared for by my mother and father" (*Christianity Today,* April 1, 1977).

A modern, compassionate person would cringe with revulsion at the feeble cries of a discarded baby, and yet can walk past our sterile, antiseptic hospitals where abortions are performed en masse. What has happened to people from a so-called Christian culture? What should our stand be today in relation to the wholesale bloodletting which is a legal part of our American jurisprudence?

In 1975 there were 1,000,000 abortions performed in the United States and 3,100,000 births (*America,* September 25, 1976). This is one out of every four pregnancies which were terminated "legally." If we have gone this far in just a few years, how much longer will it take before we regard life—*any* life—as dispensable?

God knows us before we are born. The psalmist says, "You made all the delicate, inner parts of my body, and knit them together in my mother's womb. Thank you for making me so wonderfully complex! It is amazing to think about. Your workmanship is marvelous—how well I know it. You were there while I was being formed in utter seclusion! You saw me before I was born and scheduled each day of my life before I began to breathe. Every day was recorded in your Book" (Psalms 139:13–16 LB).

When God spoke to His prophet Jeremiah, He said, ". . . I knew you before you were formed within your mother's womb; before you were born I sanctified you and appointed you as my spokesman to the world" (Jeremiah 1:5 LB).

If the Bible lays down principles, what does science say about the formation of life? The really crucial moral debate comes over whether the fetus is a human life, and when does human life begin? If the fetus is actually human life, then abortion has profound moral and legal implications.

Medically, it has been proven that by the time a woman suspects she is pregnant, there is no question that a distinct human life is growing within her body. Dr. Kenneth Mitzner says that by the fourth week after conception the heart is beating, the three principal regions of the brain have begun to differentiate, and all other organs are present in at least primitive forms. (*Christianity Applied*, November, 1974).

When does an abortion usually take place? It is rare for an abortion to be performed less than six weeks after conception. A woman tends to wait for a second missed period before going to a doctor, especially if she doesn't want to believe she's pregnant.

"Abortion at six weeks kills a little human being with arms and legs, fingers and the beginning of toes. His head may appear outrageously large compared to his body, but this is only because of the rapid rate at which his brain is developing. At this age he will already respond, by flexing his neck and trunk, if his lips or nose are stroked lightly. His brain waves can be observed with modern electronic devices," reports Dr. Mitzner.

There are two ways to kill a baby at this age. In a dilation and curettage, the abortionist reaches into the womb with a sharp instrument, cuts the baby and his associated membranes into small pieces, and scrapes them out.

With the suction method, the baby is torn from the wall of the uterus by a very powerful little vacuum cleaner. The doctors who use this device refer to it by the vivid term "baby-scrambler."

There is another method which is used, if the pregnancy is beyond fourteen weeks, called "salting out"; a needle is inserted through the wall of the mother's abdomen into the body of waters surrounding the baby. Some of the fluid is removed and replaced by a concentrated salt solution. This solution draws out the baby's body fluids and sears his skin. Death is slow and painful, according to doctors interviewed.

If the details are repugnant, imagine the work of the pathologist who must examine the pieces of the fetus after a legal abortion. A doctor stated, "The doctor who does the abortion never has to look at the results of his work" (*Christianity Applied,* November, 1974). The doctor can perform many abortions during a day's work and still have time and energy for a golf game or a cocktail party.

The Bible says we are known before we are born . . . that God knew us as we were being formed in "utter seclusion." Medical science says that a little human being is formed as early as six weeks after conception. Legally today we can take that life.

Should we allow the courts to determine the moral direction of our lives? We will be held accountable for our silence!

Patti was a teenager when I first met her. She was a little girl desperately seeking love. Her father beat her for slight infractions of rules and her mother was overbearingly harsh. I spoke to her mother one time, pointing out the precious gift she had in Patti, and got only complaints about Patti's behavior in return.

Soon after graduating from high school Patti began to travel with a rock group. She was the "housemother" for the six fellows in the group. During this time she had several abortions, all of which were terrifying to her. Then Patti became pregnant and "had to get married." After her personal history of abortions, that amazed me, until I realized that she probably had found the one man she wanted and this was her way of forcing a marriage.

When Patti's baby is born, I believe she will look at her child and wonder about the previous babies who were killed in her womb.

Another young girl became pregnant and soon after she knew that she was going to have a baby, she herself was born again spiritually into the Kingdom of God by accepting Christ as her Savior. Her baby had been conceived out of wedlock, the father was not willing to assume the responsibility, and Letha was in a turmoil. I watched three young Christian girls extend themselves for Letha in one of the warmest acts of love and friendship. They were all working girls and had rented a small house to share living expenses. They invited Letha to move in with them and cared for her with loyalty and encouragement during her pregnancy. They helped her find counseling for placing her child for adoption, since she had prayerfully decided that she could not care for her baby properly and wanted him to grow up in a Christian home.

When the time came for Letha to give birth, one of her friends accompanied her to the hospital, stayed with her in the labor room and supported her with prayer and love when the baby was born.

Abortion or adoption? What are God's guidelines?

If we are believers in the Lord Jesus Christ, we have been adopted.

What an amazing and wonderful concept to realize that He chose us. He wants children.

> For you have not received a spirit of slavery leading to fear again, but you have received a spirit of adoption as sons by which we cry out, "Abba! Father!" The Spirit Himself bears witness with our spirit that we are children of God, and if children, heirs also, heirs of God and fellow-heirs with Christ, if indeed we suffer with Him in order that we may also be glorified with Him.
>
> Romans 8:15–17

God loved me so much that He adopted me. He will not take me and disown me. He will not withhold His fortune from me or give it to me temporarily and then say, "You've made me mad, Carole, you're no longer My daughter." I am an heiress!

Then along comes Satan and says, "Carole, you really blew it today. You said something very biting to that friend. You're not a child of God!" On every count, Satan is battling hard to abort us.

I really don't want to get heavy about Satan in this book about the family. However, he is very real and exists today, as he has from the beginning when he told Eve that she really didn't have to worry about dying if she just took a little bite of that fruit. Today Satan puts on the theologian's garb and tells us that it isn't important for us to believe in the literal and inerrant view of the Bible. He tells us that it isn't important to believe that Christ was resurrected bodily. Satan puts on the intellectual garb and tells us that when young people come to the seminary they have to unlearn some of these myths they have been taught in church.

It's also important for Satan to abort us before we are born again. He says, "Don't get involved in anything that you can't explain intellectually. Don't get carried away by emotion." He mocks and misuses the phrase "born again," until it can refer to anything from political ideas to an advertising scheme.

God adopts us. Satan seeks to abort us.

A nurse in an OB-GYN office recently told me that not a week goes by that someone doesn't call asking for information on babies to adopt. There are couples who have prepared in their hearts and homes a place for a child but cannot find one.

Perhaps a great deal of success of the abortion movement has been due to the overpopulation hysteria. Perhaps the world inflationary spiral has contributed to women's thinking that they just can't afford a child. However, I believe that the emphasis on women's rights (*after all, it's my body and what I do with it is my business*) and the new ethic which says we should take life when it is unwanted, diseased, or old, are the chief contributory issues in the abortion movement.

What's Your Potential?

When I was carrying my babies, I remember talking to them and wondering what they would be like. When a child is aborted normally (miscarried), God has a reason for this. None of us can answer all the *whys* in life, but God doesn't make mistakes. He just says, "Trust Me."

A living, growing human being, made in the image of God, has the potential of becoming a mother, a doctor who will discover the cure for cancer, an evangelist who will lead thousands into spiritual rebirth. A Dwight Moody or a Frederick Handel, a Leonardo da Vinci or an Abraham Lincoln could be thrown away in bits and pieces in some dingy office or sterile operating room.

At some stage in our life as a family, as children adopted by the Creator of this universe, we will be asked to take a stand on this issue.

A birth is very costly. It costs the woman discomfort, pain, and sacrifice. Birth costs the father (in today's society) a great deal of money, sacrifice, and responsibility.

A child is born! Bring on the flowers and gifts! I shall never forget the look on my son-in-law's face when he walked out of the delivery room carrying his five-minute-old daughter. The messy, unwashed, squirming little bundle was the most beautiful thing in the world.

As members of the family of God we must be positive witnesses to the precious value of life—*every* life.

Phase III

Next Generation

7

Children Sitting in the Market Place

So many other influences from the world outside pull upon their children and give instruction dramatically counter to the ideals nourished in the family . . . . Who knows, these days, what will become of children?

MICHAEL NOVAK, *philosopher and social critic*
Los Angeles Times, *May 8, 1977*

But when Jesus saw what was happening he was very much displeased with his disciples and said to them: "Let the children come to me, for the Kingdom of God belongs to such as they. Don't send them away!"

Mark 10:14 LB

You've heard of Amram and Jochebed, haven't you? They are an important couple in the divine scheme of the world, even though they are forgotten by many today. They lived in a country and at a time when conditions were so evil that children were being slaughtered under governmental orders. If they had said, "The times we live in are wicked, we don't want to bring a child into this kind of world," then a baby by the name of Moses might never have been born.

A couple in England by the name of Sam and Susanna might have said, after having fourteen children, "Enough is enough!" and consequently John Wesley, one of the greatest Christian preachers, and his brother, Charles, who wrote more than six thousand hymns such as "Love Divine,

All Love Excelling," would never have blessed the world with their talents.

Mrs. Lincoln might have said, "We just don't have enough money to have a baby."

What if we say that a child has a basic right to be born? That's a rather thought-provoking statement, except that God's Word seems to substantiate it. For instance, when God spoke through the apostle Paul in Ephesians 5, He gave some guidelines for husbands and wives. Then in the beginning of Ephesians 6, He zeroed in on children. He made the logical sequence from man to woman to child.

We have arrived at Phase III of our family journey. Children are born and parenting is not a question, it's a reality. Are we expected to sacrifice our rights for theirs? Do children have rights?

In the stages our children go through from birth to age twelve, it seems that all we hear is about their rights. First they scream for their rights. Then they tease for their rights. Sometimes they threaten, other times they flirt. They are masters of psychological motivation. They know how to play one parent against another and how to achieve their wants by appealing to parental pride. They are skilled manipulators—and yet they *do* have rights.

Grow in Wisdom

We should allow our children to be children. I can remember something my father said to a friend who was complaining about the neighborhood children shouting and laughing in a wild game of tag. "Don't quiet their laughter. They have too many years of tears ahead."

The Bible says very little about the childhood of Jesus, and yet in one full verse we learn so much about the principles of raising a child. "And Jesus kept increasing in wisdom and stature, and in favor with God and men" (Luke 2:52). Joseph and Mary were guided by God in raising this boy. Those should be pretty good guidelines. *First* He grew in wisdom.

How exciting it is to teach a child and watch him grow in wisdom! A young friend brought her little girl, age two-and-one-half, to our house and the child showed an insatiable interest in books. She followed me around, wanting me to read to her constantly. She was the obvious product of a mother who took the time and patience to teach her.

Some of us have talents in certain things and naturally want to teach our children the things we know best. However, a child who is growing in wisdom should be exposed to other areas, too. Music, sports, good books, and art all contribute to the growth of wisdom. Many of us who complain about the rock of the age (not to be confused with the great hymn with a similar title) probably neglected to expose our children to the classics and semiclassics at a time in their lives when they were forming some discerning ears. (If I weren't so guilty of this myself, I would have no right to make the statement.)

However, a child naturally loves music and teaching them little songs at an early age can be done by anyone, even those of us who can't sing. Starting a child when he is eight years old in some formal music lessons, and then encouraging him at every step of his accomplishment, will pay dividends in his life even though he never becomes an accomplished musician.

A child loves to dance. Why not dance to Strauss or Lizst or even Gershwin when they're young? Why should they do the frug at age five?

Visiting art galleries on Sunday afternoon could be more profitable in a child's training than visiting a shooting gallery. Parents who enjoy beautiful paintings can acquaint their children with art and help them develop sensitivity to beauty. If we always lived in the shadow of a junkyard, how could we know whether Rembrandt was just another brand of tire chains? The Bible says, ". . . whatever is true, whatever is honorable, whatever is right, whatever is pure, whatever is lovely, whatever is of good repute . . . let your mind dwell on these things" (Philippians 4:8).

The books we have in our homes will channel our children's reading habits. Nurturing the love of books doesn't happen by accident. I was brought up with a set of books called the Book of Knowledge. Each volume became increasingly difficult in its stories and language. When our daughter was small, I can remember her sitting on her grandmother's lap and being read the same stories I had when I was a child. Both of us developed a love of books which is a continual source of excitement.

Mae Carden was a woman who knew how to help children grow in wisdom. She wrote in her delightful little book *Let's Bring Them Up Sensibly* that "Children wake up and have a terrific desire to learn at about five and one-half years of age. If that desire is not captured, they go back asleep, and the job of reawakening a desire to learn becomes increasingly difficult with each passing day."

It's fortunate that about the time the little darlings are waking up to learning, the school system says, "Let's take them." School and home should be working together for the good of the child, not separately to produce a split personality. However, many parents face a dilemma. They have been told by the government that the neighborhood schools may not be the best place for their children because they are not composed of the proper racial mixture. Increasingly, the ties between school and home are being separated.

Government cannot be God. God is color-blind, and when He gives us His eyes to see, the skin, the accent, the clothes are unimportant. When love is generated by the Spirit of God, the problems of integration can be resolved without man-made regulations and restrictions. God has also given us free wills and the freedom to work and live where we may. I believe that every freedom which is taken from us by the government of men is offensive to God.

The foundation of a child's education is laid in those first few years. In a creative society, given the right to exercise our God-given freedoms, it would seem that parents and churches could find alternatives to forced integration.

Let our children be children, free to grow in wisdom—not pawns to be manipulated by social planners.

To help a child grow in wisdom doesn't take a college degree; it simply takes a doctorate in patience and ingenuity. It doesn't take any creativity to turn on the TV and plop a child on the couch, but it does take mental gymnastics to keep him busy and happy.

Kathy is a young mother with a little girl and another baby on the way. When I walked into her house, which was fragrant with an old-fashioned aroma of baking bread, her two-year-old, Mandy, was busy with a cardboard stove and little pans, baking up a storm. Of course, Mandy doesn't stay busy too long at one thing—her attention span is about as long as her little finger—but Kathy was prepared mentally for the next challenge.

Today it takes God's wisdom to choose toys for a child. Television touts the latest sex symbol doll or the newest windup (breakable in a week) robot, and we succumb because of the pressure. Let them be children. Why should bosomy dolls urge little girls to grow up before they are ready? The desire to be grown up and teeter around in mommy's high heels and jewelry is a natural fantasy. But when a fantasy is urged by overeager parents, we see some of the results today.

Good Housekeeping (August 1977) published an article entitled "What Are They Doing to Our Children?" When young TV and movie stars, hardly in their teens, use obscene language, engage in off-beat sex, and commit murder on the screen, it's time for parents to object! Three of the current teenage stars, little girls with tremendous talent, have played the roles of a child streetwalker, a demon-possessed child "shrieking the most obscene language ever heard on the screen," and a con artist. Off-beat sex on TV and the movies is being used by the "legitimate" television and filmmakers, and yet the cry about child pornography is building to a mounting shout. Where will it end?

A child has a right to be a child.

Grow in Stature

The Bible doesn't give us specific verses on some areas of child raising, but principles to apply. When Jesus grew in stature, strong enough to build the kind of health required to live in the desert, walk for miles over the hills of Judea, His mother must have made certain His lunch was one that could sustain Him. Today we are hearing a lot about nutrition, and many parents are giving their children their natural birthright to good nutrition. I watched one mother give her small child a concoction which looked like peanut butter balls as a snack. It was made up of peanut butter, honey, wheat germ, and nonfat dry milk. From a nutritional standpoint, it was certainly superior to the ingredients of the cookie jar, which I must admit still resides on my countertop.

Fresh fruit and vegetables are less expensive and have better value than all the convenience foods. If a child rejects some food, disguise it. The responsibility of meal preparation and food buying is traditionally left to the woman. We all get bored with the day-to-day activities, but perhaps we should consider the alternative to that type of boredom.

Can you imagine how tiresome it would be to eat the same thing day after day, year after year? No variation, no gourmet cookbooks, no anticipation of a different meal. Imagine what it was for the Israelite mama, who tramped around in the wilderness with her husband and children and a few thousand other Jews that God led out of Egypt. For forty years all they had was manna, which was like wafers and honey. ("Here's your manna today, children—don't leave any on your plate.")

Learning about proper food selection and preparation is not enough. We need to eat at certain times and share meals together. Many husbands get home later than a child's dinner hour can accommodate. It's important, however, even at an early age, to sit around the family table together, to teach a child from a very young age that table conversation is fun and that table manners are important. I realize that mom and dad need time to talk—time to romance—at dinner. However, some of the greatest learning times are around the supper table.

Grow in Favor With God

As Jesus grew in wisdom and stature, He also grew in favor with God. He grew mentally, physically, and spiritually. Some parents do not give their children spiritual sustenance and therefore deny them one of the essentials of their basic rights. We are mental, physical, spiritual, and social beings. If we believe our child should go to school, see the dentist and the doctor, take music and tennis lessons, but let him "decide for himself" about his spiritual growth, then we are crippling our children.

Even Christian parents reach a period when they say, "Johnny just doesn't want to go to Sunday school, so I won't force him." I don't have pat answers to this issue, but I can tell you what we did that worked.

When Kent, our second child, began to balk at Sunday school in seventh grade, it was because he said he couldn't relate to his teacher (those weren't the words he used—I believe it was something like "I can't stand her"). We felt Kent was testing us, not the Sunday school. We began to discuss the teacher, all of her good points, and squelched any negative remarks about her. He continued to go to Sunday school, not because we "forced" him, but because it was the only acceptable thing he could do. We were in Sunday school or church, and he had to be in Sunday school or church.

How can a child be forced to go to Sunday school if his parents are there, too? The most important gift a parent can give to his child is the assurance of the gift of salvation. I don't care how beautiful, how smart, or how popular a child is, unless he knows Jesus Christ as his personal Savior, he cannot be a complete person.

A child longs for spiritual knowledge. He looks to us for answers to his complex questions. Can we answer him?

"If God is so big He made the whole world, how can He live in my heart?"

"Why did God make blind people?"

"Is God mad at me?"

"If Jesus had long hair, why won't you let me?"

How old should a child be before he can be born again spiritually? A child can comprehend spiritual matters long before we think he can. In Corrie ten Boom's book *In My Father's House,* there is a chapter entitled, "Five Is Not Too Young." Your child may become a child of God at a very young age if you tell him first that God loves him. Then explain that God sent the only child He had, Jesus, to live on earth and to die so that all of the naughty things we have ever done or will ever do are forgiven. Ask your child if he would like to thank God for His Son, Jesus, and ask Jesus to lead him and be with him always. Then talk to God in prayer . . . something like this: "Thank You, God, for Your Son, Jesus. I love You, Jesus. Please come into my heart and be with me always."

"And where is Jesus now?"

"Jesus is in my heart."

"Will He ever leave you?"

"No."

"And that's what the Bible means when it says 'fear no evil, for I am with you.' That means Jesus is with you."

A gracious God is not going to allow a little child to be lost in eternity if he dies before reaching what is called the age of accountability. When the Scriptures say that Jesus told the disciples to let the children come to Him, He meant just that.

Grow in Favor With Man

In the one-verse description of the childhood of Jesus, it says that He also grew in favor with man. He grew socially.

In the childhood stage, there are times when all of us think we are raising little monsters. Anyone who piously asserts that man is basically good has never raised a child. We've come a long way from the proper society of Emily Post. Too long. In this era when we hear so much about return to nature, why don't we initiate a return to good manners? A Christian home has an Unseen Guest constantly present. With a guest of this importance, our dress, attitude and our manners should be the best.

From childhood, our children can be taught how to address their elders. They can be shown principles of cleanliness, they can begin to learn how to handle their silverware, how to eat and drink.

All children are different and some are so much easier to teach to be civilized than others. Most of us think that it gets easier with each child. It's not that the child is easier, it's just that we have more experience. The first child is the Grand Experiment, the second is the Mistake Corrector; after that, your guess is as good as mine.

The Right to a Christian Home

The disciples of Jesus were like some secretaries I know. They are so dedicated to protecting their boss from unnecessary intrusions that sometimes they shut out the very persons he should see. At the height of Jesus' ministry, people wanted their children to get near Him, to touch Him or listen to what He had to say. The disciples said, "Keep those kids away from Him, can't you see He's busy?" But Jesus said, "Don't stop the children from coming to Me. The kingdom of heaven belongs to them."

Children have a right to come to Jesus. They have a right to a Christian home. What   hould be in that home? Do they have a right to a television set, a ten-speed bike, a room of their own? All of those things are nice, but the most important ingredient in that home is *love*—happy, loving parents, if the child is fortunate enough to have two living parents. Even a very small child can pick up the tone of anger between Mom and Dad. A slammed door is a universal signal of a temper. When a child is small, he can't escape from a home with tension and discord. However, when he passes into the age when an escape is possible, he may bolt.

Kids should have acceptance and appreciation. It's one thing to tell an adorable toddler, "My, you're the sweetest little girl," and another thing to find something positive to say to a gawky eleven-year-old with braces and stringy hair.

Casual criticism can destroy a relationship. One of our children came home from visiting a friend and wouldn't eat for two days. I nearly went frantic trying to figure out what was wrong until he finally blurted out, "Do you think I'm fat? Penny's mother thinks I am."

Jesus accepts us as we are. We reject people as they are. Jesus appreciates that we fall down, brush ourselves off, and stand up again. There would be no reasons for Romans 8:28 if we had perfect natures.

When I was growing up I was not attractive and I was frequently told so. My mother was very pretty, small and had naturally curly hair. My father was a big Swede with a large nose and a stomach to match. I frequently heard, "My, you look like your father." Although I loved him very much, I didn't really want to look like him!

However, my father appreciated me very much and constantly sought ways to show it. He gave me responsibility beyond my years. I'll never forget the time he gave me a very precious diamond ring to carry down to Sol, the jeweler, to have appraised. My dad was always making business trades, and this was one of them. With each step toward the jewelry store the little black velvet box seemed to get larger and larger. I was sure it had a neon sign on it which flashed: **I'm a diamond . . . steal me!** I made it to the jewelry store and back without a mishap. My father had given me new self-esteem by entrusting me with such a large responsibility.

Why is it that parents talk in front of their children as if they're deaf? Some kids are downgraded, humiliated, and criticized in a way we would never do with a respected adult.

Sometimes I think it's just as bad to compliment and praise children in front of others. In the great love chapter in 1 Corinthians 13:4, Paul says that love is not proud. "Do you mean I shouldn't be proud of my children?" Certainly pride has its place. But if we put our children on an impossible performance basis by saying, "Johnny is such a good student, I know he's going to make all *As* this year," poor Johnny is squirming inside, wondering if he can live up to our expectations.

One of my best childhood friends had a father who was inordinately proud of her. Kitty was the oldest of three girls and every time her father was around her—particularly in a group situation—he would put his arm around her and brag about her accomplishments. Poor Kitty would shift from one foot to another and be excruciatingly embarrassed. Our high-school crowd broke up and went away to college. When we met again during the Christmas holidays, Kitty was at one of the round of holiday parties and indulged in too much rum punch. She became rip-roaring drunk and then painfully sick. When we were able to deposit her at home, her father received the poor girl with unleashed fury at all of us who brought her home. He knew that Kitty could do no wrong, and he blamed the entire incident on us.

If we elevate our children too high and they slip—which is inevitable—they may stop trying to climb.

What are the ways we can show acceptance and appreciation? I think physical touch is so important. If a child is hugged and kissed when he is small, it won't be so difficult to make the transition when he is older. Little boys, especially, reach the point when to be hugged is so painful. I hugged my boys when they were totem poles, stiff and unmoving and making funny faces. In some families it seems too difficult to be warm.

We have a new bumper sticker which is questioning us from the back of many cars today. It says, HAVE YOU HUGGED YOUR CHILD TODAY? At first I thought that was a redundant question, like, "Have you brushed your teeth today?" or "Did you get out of bed today?" Then it occurred to me that if the question even has to be asked, there may be many families who need the reminder. There is a proverb which says, "Do not withhold good from those to whom it is due, When it is in your power to do it" (Proverbs 3:27).

Right to Be Disciplined

In a Christian home children have a right to be disciplined. What should our parental attitude be? Should we be of the permissive school or should we be the stern authoritarians? I believe the word *discipline* can encompass both views, but it must be balanced by the greatest training tool of all—and that's love. The proverb says, "Train up a child in the way he should go, Even when he is old he will not depart from it" (Proverbs 22:6). A soldier cannot be trained without discipline. A skilled worker in any profession will never advance without discipline. A busy street must have STOP signs. Some people have better disciplined dogs than they do children!

To spank or not to spank, that is the question. In these days of extreme child abuse, the thought of "corporal punishment" sends chills through some parental spines. The Bible says, "He who spares his rod hates his son, But he who loves him disciplines him diligently" (Proverbs 13:24). Nowhere in the Bible, however, does it say to take up a switch and correct a child every time he disobeys.

When God deals with us He uses a variety of ways. He doesn't hit us every time we misbehave.

I was brought up to believe that every time something happened to me which was bad, like falling off my bike and skinning my knees, or getting sick, that somehow God was punishing me for something which I had done wrong. My childhood concept of God was a harsh judge giving me a real whammy when I was naughty.

Dr. Bruce Narramore says in *Help! I'm a Parent,* "I believe the biblical approach is to utilize a variety of corrective measures and to spank only when necessary and then only in love." A spanking may be only the way of venting a parent's anger, and it can be badly abused. Age also has a great deal to do with a spanking or not. A small child cannot be reasoned with, but he can understand a little slap on his hand when he's getting into forbidden territory. However, physical correction is sometimes used too quickly and without thinking through to the best way of correction.

I get furious when I see a parent slapping a child on the face. However, I can remember slapping Kent when he was about six or seven so hard that his cheek turned bright red. I was so sick about what I had done that I cried for hours and then begged Kent's forgiveness.

A woman came into my house one day with her four-year-old boy and I inwardly cringed over what I knew would be the little path of destruction he would leave. He was pulling on our cat's tail when his mother said, "Now, Peter, don't do that, darling." With that, darling Peter kicked her in the shins. She reached down to rub her leg and pretending to cry a little said, "Peter, see how you hurt Mommy?"

I said, "What are you going to do when he draws a gun on you when he's sixteen?"

I insulted and shocked her so thoroughly that she left with darling Peter and I didn't see her again for several months. When she came over again I was amazed at the change. Peter stood quietly by her side. He didn't get into anything, and she didn't have to scold him once. When they left, I rewarded him with an apple and told him to come again. And I meant it. His mother said—very significantly—when they left, "Thank you for what you said to me."

Many of today's homes are suffering because of lack of discipline. Some people seem to think that when a request is refused or when misconduct is punished, it shows a lack of love. When we don't equip our child to face the demands of life with discipline, we are denying him one of the rights he has in a Christian home.

The Bible has several stories about what happens when parents don't discipline their children. David had a son called Adonijah and he was a handsome boy. David probably looked at this fourth son of his and said, "He's so good-looking, I just can't bring myself to punish him for anything." In 1 Kings 1:6 it says, "And his father had never crossed him at any time by asking, 'Why have you done so?' " So the spoiled, handsome son rebelled against his father and tried to take over his throne.

The same thing happened to the house of Eli because of his failure to be a strong father. The Lord told Eli that because of the sins of his sons, judgment would fall upon Eli's house. The Lord put His finger on Eli's weakness when He said, "For I have told him that I am about to judge his house forever for the iniquity which he knew, because his sons brought a curse on themselves and he did not rebuke them" (1 Samuel 3:13).

Children learn discipline from their mothers and fathers. If a child-care center or a baby-sitter is in charge for hours out of every day, then the parents or parent should be certain that loving and proper discipline is being used with their child.

Who's in Charge Here?

Long before I had heard about the sturdy "chain of command" idea, it seemed logical to me that a God who could design the intricacies of nature and the universe certainly knew better than I did how to raise a family. The foundation is there for every home; it only baffles me how we want to build on shifting sand. With Jesus Christ at the head of our family, appointing His second-in-command as the father, who in turn delegates the responsibilities to the wife, what do we do with the children?

First, watch over them with vigilance. Anyone with a small child knows the constant parent radar which says, "I must check and see where he is now." However, that vigilance must continue so that we know where our kids are, who they are with, and what is expected of them.

We must help our children find God as soon as possible. The little sponges are so receptive to what we give them.

The next thing we need to do is keep our children busy.

Yesterday my two little friends who play beneath my study window, Christa, age six, and Bobby, age four, came over to my house, each carrying a paper plate which was appropriately decorated with their own drawings, and on each plate were some cookies. I relished those cookies because their creative mother was directing them into doing something useful.

Our homes should be the central attraction for our children. When they walk in the door they are home safe. If there are no children in our own home, I believe that children of other families also have the right to support from the body of Christ. We have a coffee hour between services at our church. It's so comfortable to talk to our friends, stick with our own families. What would happen if the children began to feel that other adults in the congregation cared for them? The Bible says to encourage one another, and a child who is encouraged will grow and develop and be a joy to himself and to all who know him.

In the Market Place

In each generation the elders shake their heads and say, "What's the world coming to?" Jesus said the same thing of His time: "But to what shall I compare this generation? It is like children sitting in the market places, who call out to the other children" (Matthew 11:16).

What did He mean? He was comparing the controversies of His generation to the play of peevish children. One group wants to play one game and the others want to play something else. When they can't agree, they say, "Forget it, I didn't want to play anyhow."

Today, our children sitting in the market place of the world don't know what to play. They are pulled by this force, pushed in another direction, and ricocheted against the walls of confusion. The results are children who run away, become socially or spiritually maladjusted, or resort to crime.

A national survey indicated that the American home is the most violent place in the country! The study "led researchers to conclude that physical violence occurs between family members more often than it occurs between any other individuals or in any other setting except for riot and war" (*Santa Monica Evening Outlook,* February 25, 1977).

It's not easy to be a parent. In fact, it is the most demanding, creative, and exciting job in the world. We try to teach our kids one thing, the world tells them another. It's like being an artist. We search the past and attempt to learn from the masters, but we use contemporary materials on the canvas. The creative artist-parent works when he doesn't feel like it, continues when he feels discouraged, and persists when he wants to give up.

Since the world has a way of getting into Christian homes, we can reverse the process and put more of our homes into the world through our children. A little child will lead them.

8

No Problem Kids

I'm scared to death. What if I should give birth to a child who was blind . . . or deformed . . . or mentally deficient? I don't know how I could cope with that.

Remarks of a pregnant woman

If you had a Rembrandt all covered with dirt, you wouldn't take it to a car wash to be cleaned up—you'd take it to an expert. I feel honored that we have been entrusted with kids that others thought were "less than perfect."

Mother of six adopted "cast-offs"

The gaunt, starved face of a child, belly bloated with malnutrition, stares at us accusingly from the advertisement. Perhaps we write a check hastily and send it to the fund, our guilt feelings allayed for a time. Some other country, some remote part of the world, we think. It doesn't affect me.

What if I should have a child who was born blind, deformed, or mentally deficient? What if something should happen to my child that would leave him with less than a good mind or body?

Most parents have times when they think their kids are a real problem. They wonder if they will ever have the wisdom to raise these complex creatures. How would you like to raise six kids who tumbled into your life in six years, five of whom who had emotional or physical problems?

Meet the Southards. Becky and Ray chose their children, which is something those of us who are natural parents can't do. They chose the unwanted, the difficult, and the cast-off. Any one of their children could have presented a staggering problem, but the Southards multiplied the challenge by six.

Becky was a young wife who wanted a child. When she discovered she couldn't have children, she began to develop feelings of self-doubt. She said, "I wanted to die. It seemed God was trying to punish me or tell me I was unworthy to mother a child. We were turned down by every adoption agency because our religion was a 'psychological crutch,' or so the social workers said. We weren't parent material, according to them, and it seemed to me that God thought so, too."

In a world where there are so many unwanted, abused children, it seems ironic that for years Ray and Becky were unable to adopt a child. Becky prayed, and she cried. The only thing she ever really wanted to do, the only success she ever wanted, was to be a good wife and mother. Her self-image was crumbling. "I saw women who were promiscuous, and having children all the time. What was the matter with me?"

It was New Year's Eve at a candlelite service in church when Becky gave up. She said, "I told God, 'I give up. Whatever it is You want, God, I'll accept. Just let me know what You want for me.' "

A few months later a lawyer called and asked the Southards if they wanted a baby girl. Amy came into their lives at that time, and in the next six years, five more—who were considered unplaceable—joined the family.

Come Meet the Family

Joshua is the youngest. He is one of the airlift babies who was brought out of Cambodia in 1975 when that little country fell to the Communists. On one of the last planes able to escape, there were nineteen children who were in such deplorable shape that the authorities thought they had no chance of survival if they remained.

"Even if we didn't have any other kids, the miracle of Joshua would be worth it," Ray Southard said.

When Ray and Becky saw this sorry little bundle of humanity, it was estimated that he was fourteen months old. He was blind, extremely malnourished, had internal parasites, tuberculosis, double pneumonia, and suffered extreme trauma. He had never eaten anything but strained baby food, and when they took him home he was so hungry he threw up everything he was fed.

Why did Ray and Becky take Joshua? It was simple. "We were the only people who said they would accept a child who was blind."

When I first met Ray and Becky, they came to my home and brought

Joshua with them. At that time he was an adorable little boy of three, playing quietly on the floor with his toy cars as we talked. His mother showed him a book and he picked out all the pictures by name. He looked at the squirrel climbing in our oak tree. "But I thought you said he was blind," I said.

"Doctors have examined him and are puzzled," Becky said. "He has irreversible eye damage which ordinarily would make it impossible for him to see. When he first came into our family he bumped into everything and could only distinguish light and dark. But you see him now."

Joshua came running to his daddy, deftly avoiding my cat and the sharp edge of the coffee table. Ray hugged him and ruffled his shiny, coal-black hair. "Joshua is just one of our miracles."

Amy was the first child to be adopted, and the only one who was a baby when she joined the family. She is now the second youngest in the family. She acquired four older brothers and sisters, and one younger, as she was growing up. In the midst of some of the all-consuming mental and physical problems of the other children, Amy began to exhibit traits of an opposite nature. She is a gifted child who, at the age of seven, was doing junior-high work or higher, was studying architecture and oceanography, and simultaneously showing an unusual singing talent.

"Every child in our family is very special. With Amy, we try to give her an environment where she can reach her potential."

Rachel is the next oldest and was five and one-half years of age when she was chosen by the Southards. When she was born there probably was an oxygen cutoff which caused minimal brain dysfunction. She has perception and coordination problems. Rachel is an overachiever. She tries hard to do things well and wants to be a wife and mother. Her mother says she is an exceptional homemaker.

As I learned more about the children I wondered if they would be disturbed by having their stories told. Becky and Ray have an answer to this which taught me more than dozens of lectures on raising children.

"They feel so secure they are able to talk about the problems they had very freely," their mother said.

When Rachel was adopted she was not alone. Her brother, Daniel, just two years older, was invited into the family at the same time. Daniel arrived with credentials which would have overwhelmed most of us. He had been in mental institutions most of his life, and one psychiatrist had given such a negative report that no one was willing to adopt him. The diagnosis on

Daniel was that he was paranoid-schizophrenic. He also had a heart murmur and was hypertensive.

The day Daniel arrived he burst into the door, ran into the middle of the floor and started going around and around in a circle, screaming all the time. Becky looked at him with astonishment, wondering if she could possibly quiet down this whirling, shrieking dervish. She grabbed hold of him, picked him up, put him on her lap, and rocked him, talking quietly to him all the time. It's not easy to rock a seven-and-a-half-year-old boy, especially when he is a flailing bundle of complexities.

Daniel had a gender identification disturbance which was resolved with the best therapy yet designed. He needed a strong father figure for personal identification and modeling. As he began to see the position of leadership Ray had in the home, Daniel began to identify more with him.

Four years later, Daniel is a very active boy, but not the psychologically confused child he was when he arrived. He is not under medication and has no special treatment. Yet just a few years ago, all the authorities said he would spend the rest of his life in mental institutions.

His father told of an incident which showed the advancement of Daniel. Each of the children are assigned certain chores and those chores must be done satisfactorily before they are assigned to someone else. Washing the dishes is a rotating task. Each child is to wash the dishes for one week and the rule is "If you don't do it well, you stay on it until you *do* do it well."

Daniel did the dishes for one week and the results were less than satisfactory. His duty was extended for two weeks, then three, and four. At the end of six weeks of dish-washing duty, Daniel finally passed the satisfaction test (not perfection, you understand, just satisfaction). His father said, "I was so proud of Daniel. He never sulked the entire time, he just stuck to it. The Daniel of a few years ago would have probably thrown the dishes."

When Greg arrived he was also five and one-half. Ray and Becky had told the adoption agency that they wanted the most difficult child to place. They got him. Greg was an undernourished, mentally retarded, emotionally confused little black boy. He could scarcely speak English and was a very sorry little piece of humanity. He had been fed baby food, canned spaghetti, and corn flakes most of the time and could not eat normal food.

Greg was accustomed to punishment and hated everyone. One of his punishments in a foster home was to stand on one foot until he dropped from exhaustion.

When he was first introduced to a normal diet, he would sit and pick at his food for hours. Becky said, "It took him three and one-half hours to eat, and by the time he was through, it was time to eat again."

Greg is now an outgoing, fun-loving boy, normal in every respect. What was believed to be mental retardation was malnutrition and neglect.

The oldest is Mark. When he came into the family, he was twelve years old, the age which most psychologists tell us is the point of no return. At twelve, we have been led to believe, the foundation has been laid for the future personality. Heaven help us if we have not established the behavior patterns before then!

Mark had spent the past few years in the home of a child psychologist who couldn't cope with him. The psychologist knew what the books *said* about child raising, but it didn't seem to work. Mark had many emotional problems, one of which was dishonesty. On the first or second day at the Southards, he took some money from a neighbor's house. The circumstantial evidence was strong, but the denials were persuasive. Becky lined up the suspects, including Mark, and said, "Okay, kids, strip down to your shorts . . . we're having an inspection."

Mark was shocked that he didn't get away with the petty theft, but he began to learn why rules are made. The next lesson came in the area of temper tantrums. The psychologist with whom Mark had lived had said, "It allows him to give vent to his aggressions." When he moved in with his new family, they said, "This won't work in our home," and walked out of the room.

Becky said that she had some friends over one afternoon and Mark served coffee so graciously that one of the guests said, "I wish I could bring up my kids like that." Becky had to stifle a laugh, knowing that this was the boy who could not be handled by a child psychologist just a short year ago.

I Couldn't Handle It

Most of us find one or two natural-born kids more than we can take at some time or another. Do Becky and Ray have some secret formula, some magic touch that is unavailable to all of the insecure, confused parents trying to raise children in our changing world?

"As individuals we weren't very strong," Becky said. Ray shook his head, puzzled that anyone should think they were Super Mom and Super Dad. "We were barely able to cope with one child when another came along," Becky continued. "You can't turn them out naturally much faster than we had them, and none of them were babies, except for Amy. Without God's help and the support of our family, I don't see how we could manage."

What Is Worse?

Parenting is an attitude. The Southards feel privileged that God has trusted them with the children they have. Becky described their gifts in this way: "If you had a Rembrandt all covered with dirt, you wouldn't take it to a car wash to be cleaned, you'd take it to an expert. I feel honored that we have been entrusted with kids that others thought were 'less than perfect.' "

Whether our kids are gestated for nine months and born in a sterilized delivery room, or sent to us with a folder of legal documents, they are an opportunity which God has given us for existence. As I thought about Becky's analogy of a priceless painting, covered with dirt, I realized that none of us really know what we have in our children. If we looked upon them as having tremendous worth, beneath all the surface problems, what a difference it would make in our attitude toward them!

Practical Principles

How does a family with lots of children manage the everyday chores? The Southards have the tasks charted and assigned to each child on a weekly basis. Naturally, there must be consideration for the ages and physical abilities. Some of the chores, particularly dishwashing, are rotated each week. The extended family of grandmother and grandfather, aunts, uncles and cousins are very important in family activities. They play together, and also have twice-monthly prayer nights together. In our modern whirling world, midst the freeways and neon of urban living, this semimonthly family prayer time is the cement that keeps their home safe.

What about Mom and Dad? I asked the Southards if they find time to spend with each other alone. Ray said that early in the evening they spend time together. "We go to our room and the kids have to handle things. We just remind them that we deserve this time together. They see us argue, too. They learn to know that we can have a disagreement and still love each other."

Families like the Southards may not be contributing to the population explosion because they are taking up the slack; however, their view is that if God didn't want us to have children, He would eliminate the biological function. Becky said, "I don't believe in abortion. I do believe that adoption is biblical. In heathen cultures people get rid of unwanted children. The only thing we have left of value is our family unit."

If we think we are capable of raising children by the book, with the help of psychologists, or with old-fashioned common sense, we may crash when we encounter a really tough trial. The best way to raise a family is with parents on their knees.

9

From Bike to Car

Another generation of troubled youth is on stage across America,
with new discontents and hang-ups less explosive but perhaps
more profound than those of the 1960's.

U.S. NEWS & WORLD REPORT
"America's Youth," July 18, 1977

I have no greater joy than this, to hear of my children walking in
the truth.

3 John: 4

One of the ways parents have instant growth is to realize that a child is leaving and a teenager is entering the family circle. Perhaps the trauma would be less if each mother and father understood the churning within each adolescent.

Remember . . .

. . . how it was to have your voice crack and have everyone laugh at the funny way you sounded?

. . . the chagrin of discovering a zit on your chin before your first date?

. . . when you discovered that you bounced in places that didn't have a bounce a few months before?

. . . how your mother embarrassed you before your friends?

. . . how your father embarrassed you before your friends?

. . . how you hated visiting relatives, or relatives visiting you?

. . . how scared you were on your first job?

. . . how lonely you felt when you hadn't been invited to the party?

Remember?

If I were an expert on teenagers, the parental population would beat a path to my door. I began my learning process of this intriguing subject when a young lady I once knew said to me in that derisive tone unique to the period when parents become very stupid, "Oh, Mother!" This is an inimitable phrase which is a part of the universal daughter-mother relationship. It has many interpretations. It may mean, "But all the other kids are going," or it could be, "You just don't understand how I feel."

When a teenager thinks his parents don't understand, he may be right. When we are a generation removed from the fast-changing society of our young people, we have to race to see where they are before we know how to apply the brakes to where they are going.

What are the wedges which have been created to widen the generation gap? Are they any different from what the present generation of mothers and fathers experienced with their parents? Today we are thrashing in the undertow of a changing value system. It pulls us into the whirlpool of contrary thought patterns.

Recently I found myself comparing my high-school years with my own teenagers. The English Lit course, for instance, is a case in point. As a sixteen-year-old, I studied the works of Shakespeare in depth. We had a teacher who made the poetry of Whitman, Longfellow, and Sandburg ring with beauty and majesty. When our oldest, Karin, was in high school taking an advanced English Lit course, I shuddered through the filthy language and depressing saga of the seventeen-year-old in J. D. Salinger's *Catcher in the Rye.* Trusting blindly in the school system and assured that my daughter was in "academic enrichment" classes, we argued quixotically with the authorities about the type of assigned reading matter. We also began to feel oddly prudish for our conservative attitude.

Then our youngest son, Keith, brought home his book for advanced English Lit and I realized that the continuing battle for the minds had not abated. It's been ten years since Karin argued for the "reality" of Salinger, and now Keith is caught in the rye with the same saga.

What Are the Changing Value Systems?

In the past two generations, we have seen changing value systems upset our society. Subjects which were not considered fit for inexperienced minds are now contained in recommended books and courses in school. Attitudes of behavior and conduct which were the norm for a civilized society have been replaced with lower standards. Mediocrity has replaced excellence in our public schools. What are some of the reasons for these changes?

Two of the strongest catalysts in this change have been the increased teen use of alcohol and drugs. The social drinking and cocktail circuit of one generation has reached down until our children are met with the temptation of a liquor bottle a little more than a decade after they were weaned from a milk bottle. A major women's magazine featured an article on "Teenage Drinking, What Parents Can Do." Dr. Morris E. Chafetz, Director of the National Institute on Alcohol Abuse and Alcoholism, said, "By whatever standards we weigh the drug situation—numbers of users, abusers, availability, dollar value, death, disease, destruction, shattered lives—alcohol is number one" (*McCall's,* June, 1976).

Here is an expert who says that alcohol is a more serious problem now among youth than drugs.

Drinking is not just the problem of the kid who loots on the streets of New York when the lights go out, but also the private-school-educated boy or girl from Princeton, Evanston, or Beverly Hills. What are the answers? The secular experts give this advice: Dr. Ross Fishman, director of education and training for the New York City affiliate of the National Council of Alcoholism, suggests in the *McCall's* article that there is a strong connection in young people "between problem drinking and feeling that there is not a close relationship with parents."

Dr. Chafetz gives some advice to worried mothers and fathers who begin to realize that all the Sen-Sen in Johnny's pockets are not because he wanted to cover up the onions on his breath. He says, "Young people . . . are seeking answers, searching for adult roles they can comfortably adopt. Most drinking by youth is a move toward adult patterns of behavior, not rebellion against parents. Because young people seek adult roles, we must be especially conscious of our actions—even more than our words. What we do, by and large, they will do."

If parents aren't drinking and using drugs, why are so many teenagers getting caught in the syndrome? A Gallup poll surveyed over one thousand teenagers and surmised, "American teenagers believe that many members of their age group are using alcohol or drugs mainly because of peer pressure to conform and to escape from the pressures of life" (*Los Angeles Times,* July 21, 1977).

"One 15-year-old ninth-grade girl said, 'People my age sometimes follow the group so they won't be outcasts. They try to enjoy themselves, but then things get out of hand.'

"A 16-year-old girl had this to say: 'Kids nowadays are not given any alternatives to drinking and drug use—there aren't any places to go or things to do. So to have fun and excitement they drink and smoke pot.' "

What are we to do with the kids who are bored with life? What do we tell the kids who vacillate between self-stimulated highs and crashing lows? The physical changes alone during the teen years are severe enough to upset the equilibrium without the additional pressures of conformity to peer pressure.

Changing Values in the Schools

We have the world's biggest educational system in the world. We spend billions of dollars in teaching methods, textbooks, and classrooms. And yet, there is a prevailing feeling of crisis within our nation's schools. Knowledge is exploding. New challenges are presented in all the fields of academic discipline. Why is there such discontent within the schools, dissatisfaction with the results of our educational system? If there is more to learn, why aren't the kids learning more?

Here are some realities of where we are:

• *Reality:* Our modern teenagers are more worldly-wise, sexually knowledgeable, and have more money than their parents did a generation ago. They are less likely to go to church.

• *Reality:* The educational system must cope with more and more young people whose family lives are in disrepair.

• *Reality:* Teenagers today have been shaped from prekindergarten by that great baby-sitter in the tube, the television, with all of its bigger-than-life realities. Statistics: By age 16, the average child will have watched TV for 12,000 to 15,000 hours—more time than he spends in school or with his parents (*Time* magazine, September 19, 1977).

Consequently, on one hand the store of knowledge is increasing, and on the other hand the educational system is in a state of disorder. We should not point an accusing finger at our educational system, however, without realizing that it is a mirror of all society.

In some cases, sending our kids off to junior-high school or high school each day is the same as opening the door of the lion's cage and saying, "Walk right in. Keep your defenses up or you may be devoured." The conflicts in value systems become major battles when Johnny and Mary are hearing one thing at home and another from their teachers.

One of our children had a teacher who was experimenting with different forms of mysticism, hypnotism, and psychic phenomena. He was a good teacher, had the kids laughing a lot because of some of his zany illustrations, and was adding poison to the laughter with his occult ideas. We decided to have a direct and friendly confrontation and invited him over one afternoon afterschool.

As we sat on the patio discussing what he was teaching our kids, we exchanged ideas and books on the subject of the occult. We gave him the biblical warnings about the occult and he provided us with intellectual arguments for his beliefs. Without a common frame of reference, we could not reach an agreeable conclusion. However, he did go home with a promise to read the book I wrote with Hal Lindsey, *Satan Is Alive and Well on Planet Earth,* so the personal involvement may have been worth the effort. There was no confrontation, just a friendly interchange.

Most teenagers will not tell their parents if they realize a teacher is giving them material contrary to what they are learning at home or church. A grade is more important than a complaint to the school authorities. However, two Christian parents, Robyn and Larry, said that they prepared their children in junior-high school and high school to be discerning about what their teachers would tell them. "Your English teacher may say that the Bible is a beautiful piece of literature, full of interesting stories and myths. If you hear something like that, just remember that she doesn't understand yet that the Bible is more than literature, that it's the Word of God."

This is just one of the ways these parents prepared their teenagers for the different value system they would encounter. They discussed that they might hear the free-enterprise system downgraded, that national heroes might be undermined, that standards and morals might be made relative. Their advice: "Warn your kids before they hear and then they'll be able to say, 'Mom and Dad told me I'd get something like that in school.' "

Lower the Age Limits

Our kids are being forced to grow up sooner and sooner. Most of the parents of today's teenagers didn't expect to be a part of the adult action until they were out of high school. For kids today, when they can drive at sixteen, in some places drink at eighteen, and get their highs on grass at any age, growing up is not a process, it's a skyrocket.

Dr. Herbert Hendin, Columbia University psychiatrist, said, "Where young people a couple of decades ago wanted just a little more in privileges than their parents had, today's youngsters want infinitely more. Like a condemned man sitting down to his last breakfast, they feel one should live every day as if it were the last. Anything done for anybody else is an obligation, a chore, and a burden, and this poisons even their own relationships with each other" (*U.S. News & World Report,* July 18, 1977).

As kids face the challenges of coping in an adult society without the experience, the maturity, and the judgment, they become defeated and depressed. They are not ready—physically, emotionally or spiritually—to make adult decisions. What happens when depression and low self-esteem step into the picture? We see the results in violence and suicide.

An international congress on suicide prevention was held in Helsinki, Finland, where one thousand experts converged from forty-five countries. "They considered the most recent available evidence and concluded that suicide is epidemic and on the increase, especially among the young" (*Santa Monica Evening Outlook,* December 16, 1977).

In the past few years we have personally known several teenagers and young adults who have committed suicide. Thousands of college students attempt suicide every year. Why? Because life looks too difficult, too bleak.

We knew a beautiful girl who was lavished with clothes, exotic vacations, and everything she wanted. At eighteen she was sent to France for schooling and when she returned, she got a job at an exclusive dress shop and established her own chic apartment. At twenty-one, she took an overdose of sleeping pills. Why? She was a girl who grew up too soon. I had watched her through the years, learning too soon, being forced into adult situations too early, and my heart cried for this lovely child who was not allowed to be a child.

In the race to get through the teen years, so many young people are given privileges before they are taught responsibilities. As parents we sigh with relief when we no longer have to hire a baby-sittter to go out, but then we leave our kids in charge with very little direction. Do we know what they are doing with their lonely hours? Do they know where we are? Have you ever called someone and had their preteens or teens answer you like this:

"Are your mom and dad home?"

"Nope."

"Do you know when they'll be home?"

"Nope."

"Is there someplace I can reach them?"

"I don't know where they are."

A few nights later the same kids may have their parents crazy with worry when they're not in and the parents don't know where *they* are.

Many psychologists and family counselors say the most difficult years from a human perspective are the adolescent years. If you're in the teens, your world is changing as fast as your body. You have different relationships with your family and friends, and sometimes they clash in the middle.

As I write this, Christmas has just passed. We had a family service in church yesterday and everyone was urged to attend as a family. Before the service began, I looked around to see where our teenager was. He was standing toward the back in the middle of the aisle talking with a friend. Thirty seconds later I glanced around and Kurt, Mark, Karen, Debbie, and Nancy had all left their seats to join the action in the aisle. If something is happening, the adolescent doesn't want to be left out.

As members of a family, we can create the atmosphere which makes where the action is the place where we want the action to be.

The family-support system during the bike-to-car stage has to be like the thread used by jewelers to make a string of valuable pearls. It has to be strong enough so the pearls won't break, but obscure enough so that it's not noticeable.

Relationships Are More Than Being Related

How a fourteen to eighteen-year-old daughter feels about her mother may have little bearing on how she feels about her ten years later. The same mother who was made for cuddling and caring seems to change overnight to her ninth grader, who finds that Mom always seems to be criticizing and setting unreasonable rules.

Appearance is one of the greatest sources of friction between Mom and her emerging vamp. Christian mothers today are faced with difficult positions on dress standards, since we must cope with the desire for conformity. If we can establish principles which are confirmed by the Bible, we are leading our children instead of shoving them in God's guidelines. The Bible says that women should "adorn themselves with proper clothing . . ." (1 Timothy 2:9). Although that doesn't say that a string bikini is taboo in God's sight, it does state the principle.

What does a mother do when her newly curvy teenager prances downstairs with more skin showing than a baby on a bear rug? If the years before have been established with rules and modesty, then Daughter will know before she hears the verdict that she cannot wear such clothes (or lack of clothes). A daughter will test her mother right up to the limit of endurance, and all the time she is silently asking to be told what to do.

If Mother has built a relationship upon love during the years before the teens, she will have to draw upon the memories of those times when her daughter "performed" willingly to every command. Sometimes, however, the faults we see in our daughters are the very things which are wrong with us. But God can change relationships and homes through scriptural principles. One of the most important is that old principle of acceptance. We need to accept our children as they are—made in God's image and loaned to us for a time to mold and develop.

When Karin was in the crucial fourteen-to-eighteen-year-old stage, I found it difficult to accept her concept of friends. She didn't run with a crowd, but established just a few close friends and poured all of her personal energies into these relationships.

"Karin, let's have a party and you invite all of your friends from school," I suggested.

"Mom, I don't have a lot of friends—I don't want a party."

"What do you mean, you don't have friends? I'm sure you have lots of friends at school."

"Not many you would like, Mom."

I knew what she meant. That conversation took place in the turbulent sixties when political activists on both sides were violent in their reactions. Some of Karin's friends were nurtured in the liberal attitudes of their parents. We were working hard on the Goldwater-for-President campaign and the mention of the left brought sparks into the quietest discussion. Karin did not want to be embarrassed in front of her schoolmates by her parents' political leanings.

I wanted my daughter to be in the social swing, because I love people and lots of friends. She wanted to be her own person, quieter and more devoted to just a few quality relationships.

The molding God instructs parents to do is gentle, not overbearing and demanding. Parents walk a shaky tightrope between proper direction and destruction.

Mother and Son

One boy said that the best thing about his mother was that she was always there. There is a time in the growing phases of most boys when silence is more than a virtue—it's a way of life. You begin to think that a brain block has been established in the learning process which stimulates a vocabulary.

"What did you do in school today?"

"Nothin'."

"How was the game last night?"

"Okay."

A mother may hear her son talk for hours on the phone, and wonder where he learned the art of conversation. Some of the best times I had with my boys were when they were learning to drive. They were so eager to take me places and practice their driving that they were caught in a situation where conversation was a necessity. I found that just "being there" on many occasions gave me the chance to find out what was bothering the boys, what they were thinking, and how they were doing.

A boy is a teen such a short time and a man so long, the mother who takes advantage of those precious years will be a rich woman.

God loaned us one son for eighteen years and then, in a flash of time and the crash of a plane one summer night, took Kent home to be with Him forever. This is the reason I want to tell every mother to cherish the time with her children. Although I am not a woman to live in the past, it's the memories which enrich the present. I love to remember eating popcorn during late night fright movies on TV, the trips we made together, and the endless jokes with no sense.

Today those times together are deposited in this mother's memory bank, to withdraw during intervals of quiet and prayer. When the race of life seems to spin in endless circles, those precious captured moments in the life of a boy allow me to anticipate briefly the beauty of an eternity, building relationships of love.

Relationships between mother and son can be the prelude to future relationships between son and wife.

Guideline: "Correct your son, and he will give you comfort; He will also delight your soul" (Proverbs 29:17).

Mothers of sons need to remind themselves that they are molding future husbands. Will he be tender and thoughtful? Will he know how to work and support himself and his wife? Will he be the spiritual leader of his family? A boy can teach his mother the importance of long-range planning.

Captured moments and long-range planning—these are magic ingredients in a mother-son relationship.

Father-Daughter

When a daughter reaches the teen years, a father can be the most important factor in her life. He will influence her for the type of relationship which is important with the man in her future. When the father is a Christian and assumes his assigned role as head of the family, the order of priority affects all relationships.

As a girl sees her father's relationship with her mother, her attitudes will be shaped for better or for worse toward the type of man she wants to marry. What can a dad do with this emerging woman he discovers in his house? Does he turn her over gingerly to his wife, saying, "I never understood girls"?

The daughter of a busy newspaper editor told me that her dad always came to her room at night and just said, "Everything okay with you?" When she left home for college she always thought about her dad at night and how reassuring it was to know he cared.

One father we know makes it a point of taking his daughter out on a "date" once a month. A girl may find her mother only tolerable but may brag about her father.

One of the greatest father-daughter relationships I know about was between Corrie ten Boom and her father. He taught her compassion, thrift, service, and tenacity. He didn't give her a lot of material possessions, but the inheritance from her father made her one of the richest women in the world. They didn't live in a big house, and yet the few little rooms in Haarlem, Holland, where Casper ten Boom raised his family, have been visited by thousands of people. He never became famous, and yet he has taught more people the value of life through his loving relationship with his daughter.

Guideline: ". . . then you shall transfer his inheritance to his daughter" (Numbers 27:8).

Fathers of daughters need to remind themselves that they are transferring their inheritance and helping to mold future wives.

Father-Son

Somewhere in the past generation the trend has been that a father must be a pal to his son. That is only part of the father-son bond. If that relationship persisted, we would have all fathers being buddies instead of fathers. A father is a person who has authority in the family to make decisions, to guide his sons, to set an example. When my husband was growing up, his father was a banker. He looked so much the banker role that he was chosen to be in a bank advertisement in *Time* magazine. Ward was a kid with motorcycles and airplanes in his blood and steel springs in his bones. He was as charged as his dad was composed, as unconventional as his father was conventional. He respected his father, admired him, but they were not pals. The relationship was never any less for the fact.

The time a father spends with his boys is the guarantee he is making for the future. A boy needs a dad he can depend upon, a father whose integrity he does not question. A boy needs a dad who will back him up when he's in a tight place. He needs a dad who will take time to teach him a skill or listen to a problem. A mother may be tender, but a father teaches tenacity. A mother may give sympathy, but a father provides understanding.

When a boy is little, his hurts can be kissed away by his mother, but when he's almost a man, the pain requires the arms of a dad. To see a man embrace his son and say, "It'll be okay, son," is an earthly picture of the heavenly Father:

For it is He who delivers you from the snare of the trapper,
And from the deadly pestilence.
He will cover you with His pinions,
And under His wings you may seek refuge . . . .
Psalms 91:3, 4

There's probably no greater story of a father-son relationship in all of recorded literature than that of the prodigal son in the Bible. Although the parable is told by Jesus to illustrate the forgiving nature of God, it has basic guidelines for fathers today.

All sons aren't runaways, of course, but a boy may want to mentally escape from his father's authority. The father of the prodigal son forgave him, although he had every right to resent what his son did. He also welcomed him enthusiastically and treated him with compassion. The father brought him into the house, keeping those valuable lines of communication open.

In the parable, equal billing should go to the pardoning father and the prodigal son.

A father wants his son to follow in his footsteps, but only if he (the father) has made a good impression.

A Teen and His Friends

During the teen years the outside relationships become more important than they were at the primary-school level. Being accepted by others, running with the crowd, being popular, are vital. Parents should have a guiding hand on these relationships and can help their kids develop discernment.

Perhaps one of the most important searches for parents during their offspring's teen years is the search for the right church. While children are still small, parents should be looking at the youth program. Is it stimulating? Do they have Bible studies that the kids go to voluntarily? Are the people in charge attuned to the needs of the teen years?

Several years ago our church created a teen room called "The Way Inn." In adult eyes it's a scruffy room. Mismatched rugs are spread on the floor; the walls are hung with various plaques and posters; there's an assortment of chairs and couches which have seen better days. It's a great place to gather, to rap, to let the guitars and voices sing out. If every church had a form of a Way Inn, there would probably be less kids who were "way out."

The "wrong crowd" is a prevailing concern for every parent. A home can create a warm climate for friends or it can be a chilling factor. A church home can do the same.

How do you have family security in these changing times? First it is through relationships of love and then through the result of love, which is discipline.

Discipline While There Is Hope

In one of those carefully contrived "casual" conversations, I asked Keith what were the traits he most admired in his father (I didn't think it would be fair to ask about me). His answer left me with my mouth open, which is not the most attractive way to react. Our teenager said, "I think the best thing about Dad is the way he disciplines me." He may have regretted that he ever said that, because he gets reminded when the use of the car is denied or he has to be in by 9:30 on a particular night. But he said it.

Proverbs says, "Discipline your son in his early years while there is hope. If you don't you will ruin his life" (Proverbs 19:18 LB).

The kids who aren't disciplined are the overloved and the underloved. For both kinds of kids the most difficult word in the world is the word *no.* Also, for a parent to say no and then admit the mistake of the decision is a hard task. A decision made in haste is not always a good one and when a parent can say, "I was wrong, I've changed my mind," once in a while it doesn't take away the authority of the parent, but makes him or her more human.

Guidelines provide a teen with the escape hatch he needs. When a kid says, "I can't do that, my dad would kill me," what he may be saying is, "Whew, I'm out of that mess."

What forms of discipline are used successfully for teenagers? Gwen, who had two teenage girls and a boy, said that denying certain privileges was the most effective discipline. She also said that she was always available for late-night talks. Most of the time they were late night "listens" on Gwen's part while her girls or boy let the words spill.

Discipline can be laced with humor as well. Our second boy left a trail of socks, underwear, and assorted items of clothing wherever the compulsion of dropsy struck him. In complete exasperation, I took all of his assortment of wearing apparel and draped them around the light post in the front yard where he and his friends would see them when they came home from school. It was very effective.

Importance of Being Important

People need to feel important and teenagers are people. Sometimes they are treated like isolated sociological phenomena to be dissected, analyzed and programmed. Our children need to do something important! They need to feel needed, useful and have a sense of accomplishment.

Dr. Urie Brofenbrenner, child development expert from Cornell University, says, ". . . We don't let our children do anything important. Maybe they take out the garbage, but that's it. They're useless because we have made them useless. They have no experience in being responsible for other human beings" (*Psychology Today,* May, 1977).

The survival of the family depends upon its being a community, or a group of individuals working together for a common goal. One family may make a project of building a wall or planting a garden. We know a family whose "thing" is cars. They are always pulling apart, fixing up, and putting back together cars for resale. The teenagers have a sense of accomplishment. Home is the only place where it can be taught that life isn't "doing your own thing" but "doing things for others."

Jan, who has five children ranging from six to eighteen, has one night a week devoted to "kids' cook-in." They each take a turn on Wednesday planning and preparing the evening meal. When it's the youngest's turn, they may eat hot dogs or cheese sandwiches, but it's his culinary achievement. There's only one girl in that family, so you can imagine the valuable cooking experience the boys are getting.

There is no stage we go through in which we do not need a sense of importance, and the teen years are no exception.

Importance of Models

Who are the heroes and the heroines for the junior-high and high schoolers? We've come a long way from Louisa May Alcott and Jack London days. Heroes used to be bigger than life, now they're lower than life. The models the kids have are also molders of their personalities and attitudes.

Young men and women, single or married, looking for ways to serve the Lord, would do well to consider the influence they could have upon young people in the junior-high age. These kids are looking for someone to be their model for behavior, clothing, and language. If these kids are treated with respect and directed into activities by a young adult, not more than ten years removed from the scene, what a difference it could make in their futures.

Parents who are concerned about these important years can promote relationships between their kids and young adults who provide healthy modeling. One mother said, "I prayed specifically for five adults—one adult who would take each of my five kids under his wing." The Bible says to make every request be made known to God, and certainly there could be no prayer that would reap more of a blessing than to ask, "Lord, bring a young man into my son's life who loves You, and will be interested enough in my son to spend time with him." Or, "Dear God, there must be a girl who will teach my daughter through the beauty of her life. Send her to us."

Christian parents today should be looking for the activity, the church, where their preteens and teens will have the opportunity to be a part of a program which meets their physical, social, and spiritual needs. How desperately we need imaginative youth ministers, young men and women who love Christ and love those kids who need models as they change from bike to car. That position should be the most important in the church!

Teenage Fallacies

There's an organization which has as its slogan, "There's no such thing as a bad boy." That's a comforting sentiment but totally false. We are born sinners, separated from God and susceptible to every vile and dirty act which man has conceived. Adam and Eve walked in the Garden with God, and yet one of their sons murdered his brother. David was a man whom God loved, yet David wanted another man's wife and plotted to have the husband killed. We all fall short of what God wants us to be, and to say that bad kids are a result of environment, wrong color, or poverty is to discount the fact that all of these external factors have always been present and always will be. Jesus Christ can change the kids from the slums as well as the Johnny-do-no-wrong from Iowa. But, please, don't say we're all basically good.

A second teenage fallacy is that the teen years are the happiest years of your life. They are torturous for many. Psychologist Kenneth Keniston of MIT said this about America's youth: "They're turning much more inwardly to their own psyches—something we seldom saw in the 1960s when youth was turning outward to change society. Today, they're more likely to get depressed, more likely to be down on themselves, more likely to worry about how well they're doing" (*U.S. News & World Report,* July 18, 1977).

The teen years are years of stretching, in all aspects of living. Some days that stretching may be painful; other days it may be pure exhilaration. It's not easy for kids this age to look out for others and emerge from their self-imposed cloister. Perceptive adults can help penetrate that cocoon with a communications device which was invented before the electronic age. It's called . . . *listening.*

Listening isn't usually done at a convenient time—it's when it's inconvenient. God never told us He would give us children for our convenience. He said they are gifts. ". . . they are the seed of the blessed of the LORD" (Isaiah 65:23 KJV).

Heartbreak or Heartwarm Kids?

We hear a lot about the duties of parents, the perils of raising teenagers, and all the other admonishments about parental responsibilities. However, there is another side of the diminishing coin. The Bible gives some principles for kids which will provide the basis for harmony in our homes. There is a saying that little children won't let you sleep; big children won't let you live.

Teenagers have responsibilities which boost them toward responsible adulthood. One is to "Obey your parents in the LORD, for this is right" (Ephesians 6:1). One teenager asked us, "My mom and dad aren't believers, why should I obey them?" The answer is, because "this is right." Parents' judgment is not always right, but it's usually better than the kid's! Of course, if a mother or father asks a child to do something which is against God's commandment, then the direction is to obey God. "In all thy ways acknowledge him, and he shall direct thy paths" (Proverbs 3:6 KJV). God never expects one of His children to obey a parent if the parent is blatantly leading the child astray.

What a difference it makes in homes where boys and girls obey and honor parents. A home without that respect is uncomfortable and shabby, no matter how luxurious the surroundings may be.

The teenager who does not obey and honor his parents may find that an employer will not let him get away with the things he tries to get away with at home. Sloppy work, irresponsible actions, tardiness, are not qualities which contribute to job success. On the other hand, one of the greatest compliments a parent may receive is when their youngster is hired by someone who says, "He's a good worker."

Kids need to be useful. We read a lot today about the fact that kids can't get jobs, and yet in our community the owner of a gas station said that he couldn't find responsible kids to work for him. It's rare when trustworthy baby-sitters can be found.

Teenagers who learn to be responsible will never lack for work. The word *discipline* means "to be under control." Even God disciplines His children.

A visitor to America said, "The most unusual thing I saw in America was the way the parents obey their children."

What will make the changing stage from bike to car smoother, happier, more fun? Jesus Christ in a home is the answer. When Jesus was passing through Jericho, a short man by the name of Zacchaeus wanted to see Him so he climbed in a tree to get a good look at Jesus. As Jesus was going by, He spotted the man in the tree and shouted at him, "Zacchaeus! Quick! Come down! For I am going to be a guest in your home today!" (Luke 19:5 LB).

Zacchaeus's home was never the same after Jesus came. Our homes may never be the same when Jesus comes in. They will be changed!

Phase IV

Growing, Growing, Gone

10

A Time to Search

Why can't we hurry up and find absolute truth at 21? . . . The best of all parents have not shielded us from wrestling with the problems of security, acceptance, control, jealousy, rivalry.

Gail Sheehy
Passages

Let no one look down on your youthfulness, but rather in speech, conduct, love, faith and purity, show yourself an example of those who believe.

First letter of Paul to Timothy 4:12

The day we left our daughter at college two thousand miles from home was one of the most dismal experiences of my life. It was during a slushy midwestern winter and we had driven in from California. To add to my general joyless state, her steady boyfriend (who did not exactly meet our approval) had arrived from another state at the same time. Our good-byes were inhibited by his presence, and in the back of my mind I was thinking, "How long is *he* going to stay here?"

As we pulled away from the drab campus, the bare trees made me feel like some character out of *Wuthering Heights*. My poor little girl, plucked out of the warmth of her comfortable home and dropped in this bleak place. How will she survive?

I was describing that feeling to Karin almost ten years later, while we were unpacking boxes in her new home and taking turns chasing the baby. Karin looked at her own little girl and said, "I can understand now how you must have felt, but I have to admit that when you left me I felt so free and wonderful. I hope you don't mind, but I never felt homesick a bit."

107

What do we do when our kids graduate to that status called "young adult"? Turning the coin over, what do they do? When parents are reluctant to cut the strings, and young people are busy sharpening the scissors, what happens to the relationship?

Between eighteen and thirty is a stage of growing, of decision, of independence. It's a time to search. What do I do with my life? Where am I going? Who am I? These are questions we ask at every stage of life, but in this age group they dominate the thinking.

College Pressure

By the time a young person reaches the senior year in high school he has usually made a decision about college or not. If he goes on to college the shift from the high-school student mentality to the pressures of higher education may be drastic. If family has been an important life-support system, and the plugs are pulled, sometimes the patient finds himself gasping for breath. The pressures are so great.

Russ is a young man who had been more independent during his teen years than most of his peers. However, as he told me about his college experiences he said, "Most kids can't cope with the knowledge explosion. If they haven't been prepared by their parents or high school for the demands of higher education, they feel like they're caught in a torture chamber, with the walls closing in fast. Remember the scene from *Star Wars* when the fellow and his girl fell into the pit whose walls were slowly closing in on them? That's what happens to a lot of kids when they get into the college scene."

I was trying to understand what Russ was saying, but it didn't seem any different from my own college years a generation ago. And yet, I realized that what he called the "knowledge explosion" was very real and that an academic search today can be dead-ended by a new discovery tomorrow. I thought of the Bible verse which says that in the end times knowledge will increase fast and that we are "always learning and never able to come to the knowledge of the truth" (2 Timothy 3:7).

As the pressures build, many young adults begin to question the purpose of life. "What am I doing, anyhow? Does anyone really care about the way I feel?"

Who Am I?

Why is it that the number one cause of death among college students is suicide? The lack of identity, poor self-image, and sense of directionlessness squeeze an individual into the academic mold until he explodes. At a time when family ties (if there were any) are severed, our young adults need that life-support system desperately.

As I was talking about the college scene with Russ, now a seminary student (who is applying his energy and mentality to a stiff program of studies in disciplines which are stretching him to the utmost), he said, "The knowledge explosion is putting such pressures on young people today that many of them resort to psychiatry or just fall apart in the school structure."

Whether a young Christian attends a Christian school or a secular university is a matter of choice. In a Christian school the atmosphere may be more conducive to clean living, but also may lead to rebellion if the regulations are unrealistic. Eric is one young man I remember well, who fought the rules at a strict southern university. We have the results of a burning cigar on the desk in one of our bedrooms to prove it. Eric, the product of a loving, supportive Christian home, came from Europe to America to go to college. He visited our home after a semester and told us of his trips to the local bar and his glee in breaking the rules. I asked him, "Eric, did you smoke cigars and drink beer at home?"

"But, no," he said. "I never wanted to . . . but when I got to the university and had to sign that pledge with all those rules, I decided to see how many I could break."

The Christian school was telling the young people what not to do without showing them why they shouldn't. Only the strong moving of the Holy Spirit through God's Word will convince us of life's *dos* and *don'ts*. When the Bible says that our bodies are the temple of the Holy Spirit, it may take us years to realize that what we do to ourselves is polluting God's temple. That is convicting, not signing a pledge that I will or I won't do something.

In a secular college or university today, a young Christian who has been sheltered from the things of the world may be overpowered. The first encounter with a sex party, the first drink, the suggestive jokes from a professor, may send the young person from the Christian home into a tailspin.

Caught in the educational scene, propelled by the peer pressure, our young adults need to know who they are as children of God. Kit, a Christian girl brought up in a loving, secure home, said, "I wish my parents had told me that the first year of college was a course in how to drink. When it hit me, I didn't know how to react."

Parents, family, and church need to fortify our young adults and prepare them to be different. A peck on the cheek and a new Bible inscribed TO

TOM, WITH LOVE FROM MOM AND DAD isn't sufficient. Most of us think our kids are more worldly-wise than they are. We have been programmed into thinking that this generation has grown up faster, knows more, and is more capable than their parents. We are living in times when immorality is not going to decrease. It's like inflation, it can be held for a while, but then the next onslaught comes.

The real testing period on the part of parents comes when their kids come home from school for the first time. The student has tasted freedom and it's very sweet. Then Mom says, "Be in by midnight, John." And John thinks, "Doesn't she know I'm grown up now?" It's a time of great change, for all involved in the family. We are suddenly strangers.

If the principle of acceptance has been ingrained in our relationships during earlier phases of life, many hurdles can be scaled.

Quite a few of the young people from our church went to one university which is known for its liberality. Many of us were very concerned about them and prayed for them. What happened was exciting. They had a weekly core group which met for Bible study, sharing, and fun, and gave each other the support they so desperately needed as they encountered the culture of university living. They were able to build their own counter-culture in opposition to the trend. Consequently, they became stronger because of it.

What can parents do for their kids in college? Love them. Accept them. Realize that as our relationships change they will become our friends, not a burden or obligation. It sometimes takes twenty years before a young man or woman who happens to be your son or daughter becomes your friend.

I asked Robyn, a friend of mine with two girls in college, how she felt about them going away to school. She said, "Relieved. By the time they were in the twelfth grade I knew they were ready for college."

That's the way it should be. We should dig the well before the water goes dry. We should be preparing our kids for leaving home years before they do.

A person who has been brought up with a healthy regard for himself, with a knowledge that a clear mind is God's criterion for His children, will be better equipped to cope with college life.

The apostle Paul spoke to Timothy like a father to a son, and he said, "It is quite true that the way to live a godly life is not an easy matter. But the answer lies in Christ . . ." (1 Timothy 3:16 LB). Young people like a challenge. This is the reason they compete in sports, rally around a cause, and fight for a principle. I think we need to tell our kids that it takes more guts to be different than it does to conform. The principles are clear: "And do not be conformed to this world, but be transformed by the renewing of your mind, that you may prove what the will of God is, that which is good and acceptable and perfect" (Romans 12:2).

The application of the principle takes a conscious decision of the will, and the choice belongs to each of us.

Marriage or?

Between teenager and the young married are the not marrieds. One of the complaints that single young adults voice is that after a certain age, they are treated as freaks if they're not married.

Toni is an attractive Christian girl in her late twenties, active in her profession and church, and yearning to be treated as "normal." "After a time, if you're not married, people begin to treat you differently. They either try to match you up or urge you into situations where you don't want to be. Why is being married such a set-apart state?" she asked. "Why do Christians ignore parts of the Scriptures which pertain to singleness?"

It's true. We're so anxious to quote from Ephesians 5 and explain the concept of submission that we overlook great portions of Scripture which speak to singleness.

Being single is a gift. The apostle Paul was single, and said that each man has his own gift from God (1 Corinthians 7), and he considered being single a gift. This did not restrict him in providing guidelines for marriage, because those instructions weren't his, but from God. He certainly didn't say, "Look, married friends, I may not be married but I know what the rules should be." I'm sure I would never have listened to Paul under those circumstances. It would be like the maiden aunt who tells us how to raise our children. But Paul said, "But to the married I give instructions, *not I, but the Lord* . . ." (1 Corinthians 7:10, *italics added*).

Our Lord Himself was unmarried. He was married to the Church, all of those who believe in Him. The Bible tells us that Christ is the bridegroom and that someday there will be a great wedding, the marriage of Christ to the Church which is spoken of in Revelation 19:7 as the Marriage of the Lamb. This will be the most exciting wedding of all time! When Christ returns at the Rapture for the Church (please read *The Late Great Planet Earth* if you don't understand this), He is the Bridegroom coming to take His precious Bride to the home He has prepared. If you believe in Jesus Christ, you will be a part of this Great Elopement, whether you were married on earth or not.

The work of Jesus Christ on earth was done as a single man. Certainly the most unique man in all history, but, nevertheless, one who did not have an earthly wife and children.

God did not intend everyone to be married, but He does want each of us to be content in whatever state we're in—and to let others be content, too.

Corrie ten Boom is a great servant of God whose life has touched millions through her story of her family and her prison experiences. I worked with Corrie for a year on the story of her childhood and the first fifty years of her life, and was moved by her understanding of families and children in particular. It's funny, but I never thought of Corrie as being single. When she was young she was engaged to a young man, but he married someone else. It may be difficult for a Christian girl to believe that being jilted is God's will, but the ministry of Corrie ten Boom may never have extended beyond the borders of Haarlam, Holland, if she had married Karel sixty years ago.

Corrie has a beautiful English girl, Pam, working for her as a companion-secretary. Pam and I were talking about singleness, and she said that people who are single as they reach their thirties and beyond may be ready to do the best work of the Lord. She said, "I've just made myself available to the Lord and the fact that I'm not married ceases to be a concern."

Where Am I Going?

After college the career choices loom for most young adults. Some are propelled into careers by parents and find themselves chafing under the work they hate. Others are given no guidance at all and flounder for years trying to find themselves. Are there any answers to that all-important search for direction in a job or a profession?

The standards of a Christian for work should be different from those who do not know Christ. Simple questions should be asked, such as, "Is it honest? Does the company have integrity? Would I be compromising in any way my Christian principles to be associated with this company or in this profession?"

There was a case in the news about three Christian men who resigned their positions of long tenure from a publications firm because that company was printing pornography. The management argued that the men could be assigned to another publication and didn't have to be involved with the company which produced the porno. The scriptural principle, however, is that we should not be bound with unbelievers, that we should not be partners with lawlessness. Christ said, ". . . COME OUT FROM THEIR MIDST AND BE SEPARATE . . ." (2 Corinthians 6:17).

We know of a large company whose owners are Christians. They had a contract for advertising in a magazine, and when the tone of that magazine changed from a wholesome family piece to the slightly sensational, this company withdrew its advertising account.

A young man or woman does not need to compromise for the sake of a paycheck.

As the family-support system of those members who are seeking a job, a career or a business, the greatest lifeline we can supply is encouragement. So often we hear of people who did not follow their dream because it was knocked down by someone who said, "You don't want to do that, do you?" The outside world scoffs; in our families we need to boost. When others mock, we need to strengthen.

The gift of encouragement is one of the greatest gifts we can hand to our young adults. Perhaps the greatest heritage my father ever gave me was summed up in four words: *you can do it!*

After our son, Kent, was killed we began to have a succession of single young men and women living with us. It wasn't that we were seeking a way to fill a void left by Kent, it just seemed that circumstances kept sending us these singles. For a while, every time we had a cute girl living with us I tried to play matchmaker. I remember actually getting into an argument with Lynn about marriage. She said she didn't want to get married, and I was equally insistent that it was the only way God wanted us to live. It took me three years to understand that singleness is also a gift. Now I believe that one of the greatest services we can provide as a family is support for those singles whose families are far away, or who are not receiving the encouragement they need.

As Toni said, "You make me feel like a person instead of a freak."

There may come a time when our singles begin seeing double. Then the *Growing, Growing, Gone* phase adds a new dimension. From being simple mothers and fathers we become hyphenated individuals. We are *in-laws*.

11

Second Generation Jolt

Adam was the luckiest man: he had no mother-in-law.

SHOLEM ALEICHEM
(Jewish writer)

A son is a son until he takes a wife;
A daughter is a daughter all of her life.

Have you noticed there aren't so many in-law jokes recently? One of the reasons may be that families are so fragmented that in-laws are a vanishing species. They live hundreds of miles away, or the relationships are so scrambled that by the time we figure out whether someone is a step-in-law or an in-law once removed, the issue is no longer important.

A young marrieds' Bible class had seven couples who met regularly for study and social times. At Christmas, five of the couples and their small children joined some friends several hundred miles away for the holiday season. The other two couples went to their parents and in-laws for Christmas. The five couples came from broken families where the strategy of knowing who they should visit became so precarious that they decided not to visit at all. The two couples had close relationships with their parents and in-laws and couldn't imagine spending Christmas with anyone except family.

The second generation jolt can either leave charred remains as the result of the shock or provide exciting electricity to the extended family. The choice is up to us.

115

What About Parents (In-Law)?

Some people get postwedding depression. I'm speaking about the parents of the bride or groom. The goal has been reached (*whew, they're married*), the presents are stacked in the recently vacated bedroom, and Mom and Dad are catatonic. They are entering a new phase in life and it is strangely uncomfortable. What do we do now?

Ben and Gloria had anticipated their reactions to the marriage of their oldest daughter, and arranged for a honeymoon weekend of their own right after the wedding. Ben told us, "We got caught up in the romance of the whole thing and decided that we weren't going to go home and mope around about losing a daughter . . . we were going to do a little playacting and pretend it was our wedding, not our daughter's."

When our daughter was married, we decided to have a family dinner at a nice restaurant after the wedding reception. We had it planned well in advance of the occasion and had a superb time and an elegant meal. It has continued to be a family joke that while we were enjoying a beautiful postwedding dinner, the bride and groom were eating pizza from a take-out restaurant.

What happens when parents discover they are in-laws? Our practical Guidebook gives us direction by telling us first of all to plan ahead. "A wise man thinks ahead; a fool doesn't, and even brags about it!" (Proverbs 13:16 LB).

It's not easy to realize that our children are only given to us on a temporary basis. We have the opportunity to raise them, but for better or for worse, when they get married our priority in their lives slips to a lower level. God anticipated in-laws before He created them. When He said in Genesis 2:24 that "man shall leave his father and mother, and shall cleave to his wife . . ." there weren't any earthly fathers and mothers to leave. However, He had established the family in Eden and knew that when the First Family had children they would leave Mom and Dad and join with their spouses. The attitude of the parents then is not that they are no longer an important part of God's scheme—for they are important—but that their direction, advice, and authority is transferred to the new head of the family, who is the bridegroom.

Although parents may not think that the new son-in-law is prepared to be the head of his household, he will never be able to take that rightful position if his decisions are questioned, or if in-laws try to make decisions for him. The same is true for the new daughter-in-law. Parents-in-law, struggling with their new role, could do well to remember the vowel principle. AEIOU. The principle works like this: I OWE YOU . . . ACCEPTANCE AND ENCOURAGEMENT.

Do we really have to accept other people as they are? What if the son-in-law doesn't have the kind of a job which is "acceptable" in our circle? What if the new daughter-in-law is not from an "acceptable" social background?

Mothers- and Fathers-in-Law

My husband's mother made apple pies that took first prize at the church bazaars. She was a careful cook, always measuring everything precisely from a well-used recipe card. She had a particular trick she used on the crust, brushing egg white gently on it before she popped the pies into the oven. When we were first married, I dropped in at my mother-in-law's house one morning to find her in a state of extreme agitation.

"I'm having our Tuesday night couples group over tonight and they are all expecting apple pie. My day has just fallen apart and I don't have time to make them."

With all the confidence of no experience I said, "Don't worry, Mom, I'll make the pies."

She looked at me like an opera diva being told her role would be sung by the soprano in the Cartersville, Iowa, ladies' quartet. However, my mother-in-law, to my lasting endearment, said, "Bless your heart, I really would appreciate that."

She knew I had never made a pie, but she accepted my offer and entrusted her reputation to my flour- and shortening-filled hands. I managed to turn out three rather acceptable pies, and she bragged about the incident for weeks to her friends.

She taught me that even in the mundane, trivial ways in which we can show acceptance and encouragement, we will add new dimensions to relationships with our in-laws.

Naomi was a mother-in-law who had tragedy strike in a manner which would numb most of us. She had traveled with her husband and two sons from their hometown of Bethlehem-Judah to begin a new life in the Moabite hills. Her husband died, and she was left with two sons who soon married a couple of Moabite women. Not only was Naomi dealt the blow of being a widow, but also she was soon made a mother-in-law to girls who were not of the same faith. It would be like a devout Jew marrying a staunch Catholic. The Bible doesn't tell us how Naomi felt about these marriages, but the way she accepted and encouraged her daughters-in-law shows up dramatically. Both of her sons died, leaving the widowed mother and two widowed wives to fend for themselves. When Naomi decided to return to her home in Bethlehem, one of her daughters-in-law, instead of remaining in her own familiar homeland, said to Naomi, ". . . where you go, I will go, and where you lodge, I will lodge. Your people shall be my people, and your God my God" (Ruth 1:16).

What a mother-in-law Naomi must have been! Her daughter-in-law not only wanted to be with her and follow her on an unknown journey, but she also wanted to worship the one and true God of Israel, a God who was alien to her upbringing and background. Ruth had also become the spiritual daughter to Naomi.

If Naomi had seen Ruth as a threat to her, as a woman who was going to take away the love of her son, she would never have gained the love and respect she had from her daughter-in-law. If Ruth had felt that her mother-in-law was critical, demanding, or overbearing, she would never have been so willing or eager to follow her.

The comedians make jokes about mothers-in-law, but a father-in-law can be supportive or destructive, according to his personal attitude. Ted was a father who wanted such strong personal rule over his family that he was unwilling to accept the girl his son married. He was subtle, oh, so subtle in his manipulation. He never overtly downgraded his daughter-in-law, just found her weaknesses and maneuvered ways to expose them to his son. "Judy is a nice girl, son, but she seems to have a tendency to fly off the handle." Ted was like a fencer: he'd thrust and retreat, jab, and withdraw. Once in a while he'd manage to score a sharp hit and another daughter-in-law would be knocked off the pedestal, just like the kewpie dolls in the shooting gallery.

A doting father can be even more divisive when he thinks his daughter is not married to Mr. Ideal. "That guy will never amount to anything; he has absolutely no ambition." Consequently, father-in-law drives what could be a supportive relationship right into the basement.

Marrying into another family after living for twenty or more years with just one set of parents is an unsettling feeling. The mothers and fathers-in-law have not changed their roles as much as their newly married children. Perhaps the heavier responsibility should be upon the older generation to extend the acceptance and encouragement first. It could all begin with something simple . . . like establishing what the new son and daughter-in-law should call their in-laws. Will it be Mom and Dad or first names? I'll never forget the awkward moments when our new son-in-law was stumbling over what to call me. For a year it had been "Mrs. Carlson," and then suddenly we realized the relationship was going to change. I finally said, "Rick, what do you call your mother?"

"I just call her Mother."

"Then why don't you call me Mom?"

The transition was as easy as eating soft ice cream.

The most difficult lesson many in-laws have to learn is not to take sides. We hear one side of an issue and think, "You're complaint is certainly justified. You should stand up for your rights!" And then we hear the other side and think our original judgment is wrong. In Proverbs it says: "The first to plead his case seems just, Until another comes and examines him" (Proverbs 18:17).

What About Daughters and Sons (In-Law)?

The second-generation jolt hits a married couple when they realize that with the muttering of their *I dos* they have abruptly acquired a new family. All of the questions are swirling through the subconscious: *Will they like me? Will they interfere? How should I act around my new in-laws?*

One young married said that when she went to the home of her husband's parents she felt as if she should perform. "I was so self-conscious about what I said and what I did that I dreaded going to see them. This made me more tense which increased my self-consciousness and soon I didn't want to go at all." Her husband said that the atmosphere was so uncomfortable that they just began to avoid seeing his parents altogether.

In-laws are people. The prevailing atmosphere of our times may have programmed us into believing that the relationships are going to be strained. We think the problem into existence before it is there. "As [a man] thinketh in his heart, so is he . . ." (Proverbs 23:7 KJV).

Relationships are not built with the signing of a marriage certificate; they are nurtured and nourished with loving and giving. Some people seem to care for their plants better than they cultivate the precious gifts of acquired family.

One of the new decorating crazes is to have a house filled with live plants. In some parts of the country it is a flourishing business, with plant food and moisture-measuring devices developing increasing sales. We take care of our plants because we love them, not because we feel that it is a duty we have been forced to perform.

Nothing destroys a relationship more than the legal spirit of duty creeping into it. The Christian way of life was designed by God Himself to be the happiest and certainly the principles apply to our acquired family. Over the past few years I have been learning the glorious results of the "therefore" principle. Taken and applied to our attitudes it works this way:

Because God chose me to inherit all the riches He has promised His children (Ephesians 1:11) . . .

• *Therefore,* I can claim His wisdom (James 1:5) when my mother-in-law wants to come and live with us for an extended visit.

Because God loved me so much that He gave me a new life and saved me, not "as a result of works, that no one should boast" (Ephesians 2:9), but as a free gift . . .

• *Therefore,* I can love my father-in-law when he questions my judgment in choosing a place to live or accepting a new job.

Because Christ preached peace and gave me open access to speak to the God of this entire universe . . .

• *Therefore,* I can claim that peace when my heart is in turmoil over something thoughtless I have said or done.

Because God forgave me for all my sins, past, present, and future, when Christ bore them on the cross . . .

• *Therefore,* I can walk in love and forgive my in-laws (or any others) when they injure me, either purposely or unjustifiably.

I love self-help books and articles. However, many of them place us on a performance basis which is self-defeating. When we perform out of duty we may begin to chafe, feeling like a martyr. On the other hand, those acts done out of love release energy and a positive attitude beyond all of the self-motivating instructions in the world.

I have a Christian friend who writes a book with her life in the way she treats her mother-in-law and father-in-law. She respects, loves, and cares for them in the same way she cares for her own parents. She will never have to give her own children lessons or lectures (heaven forbid!) about in-law relationships. Her attitude is a lesson.

The Bible supplies that life-support in the *therefore* principle. All we need to do is to take it, apply it, and begin to live on a level which gives us the life-style that is our inheritance.

If I forget how much God loves me, I find it difficult, if not impossible, to love the in-laws and out-laws I know. But when I am reminded to "be kind to one another, tender-hearted, forgiving each other, just as God in Christ also has forgiven you . . . THEREFORE, be imitators of God, as beloved children; and walk in love, just as Christ also loved you . . ." (Ephesians 4:32; 5:1, 2).

As we're walking, we may discover that we've stumbled into something we knew was inevitable. Next phase. The phases of our lives overlap; they are never neatly divided into precise categories, waiting for us to step gingerly over the threshold. Suddenly we're there. Some of the kids are grown, some may be married, and we're a part of that age group where life is supposed to begin.

Phase V

Caught in the Middle Ages

12   Vine Ripened

12

Vine Ripened

*Of all the barbarous middle ages, that which is most barbarous is
the middle age of man.*

LORD BYRON, *1823*

. . . *O* LORD, *revive Thy work in the midst of the years,
In the midst of the years make it known* . . . .

HABAKKUK, *the prophet 3:2*

The society column in our local newspaper announced that a woman
with her doctorate in psychology, a member of a university clinical staff,
was going to speak for a large women's organization on "Woman's Midlife
Crisis."

According to chronology, I am in midlife. Since I was anxious to hear
about the crises I could expect at this crucial period, I decided to attend the
lecture.

First, we were told about the stress we were experiencing or could
expect to experience. Well, I thought, this isn't anything new. Just that
morning I had lost my car keys, answered five phone calls before 8 A.M.,
tripped over my son's skis in the front hall, and driven for half an hour out
of my way getting to the meeting. What's different about stress?

After we were told we would face stress, we were then given the defini-
tion of midlife crisis. We were told that it is the turning point, where old
ways no longer work and new ways have not been found. Many women in
the audience nodded their heads in agreement, so it was obvious she had
struck a responsive chord.

Various directions to follow were recited by the learned doctor, among
which were yoga, TM, biofeedback, and transactional analysis. She said

125

that in this era of self-help there was an overabundance of directions, and we must choose the one best suited for us. Finally, someone asked the question, "If I came to you or one of your colleagues for help for some particular crisis I was experiencing, is there something of concrete value you could give me?"

The answer was, "I was trying to avoid this. No, we do not have any one certain direction for you to take; we would have dialogue with you and help you determine your own direction."

Women were there seeking answers for real midlife problems, and they were told there were no answers.

For men or women, midlife trauma can be very real indeed. Suddenly we're there. We're caught in a squeeze play between the growing and almost-gone children and the elderly—frequently dependent—parents. We enter midlife in a youth-worshiping culture and wonder if we can hold our own in the competition.

The Middle Man

When Ben reached forty he was in a company where his future looked secure and his goals attainable. He was young enough to be aggressive, and mature enough to have stature. By the time he was forty-five, Ben seemed to be heading toward top management. He had to travel a great deal and Phyllis, his wife, could not accompany him because it was difficult to leave their three children for any length of time, especially when their fourteen-year-old daughter was beginning to show signs of sulkiness and rebellion. The harder Ben worked, the more he was gone from home, the more strained Phyllis became and the family suffered.

However, Ben was on a treadmill which couldn't stop. He had a "hurry-up" feeling that if he didn't pursue the executive vice-presidency, it might allude him. All of his life he had been a superachiever, from high-school football to college politics.

Then the company began to have serious problems. The big government contract was lost to a rival firm; one by one departments were closed and employees suspended. Ben began to see his dreams collapse with each layoff. The inevitable happened; he was suspended indefinitely and his confidence was shaken.

As Ben prepared resumés and searched for a position commensurate with what he had been earning, he discovered that after forty-five he was no longer one of the most desirable candidates for a job. His midlife crisis left him feeling unappreciated and completely valueless.

After the initial shock had subsided, Ben, a committed Christian, said that he took the verse from Romans which says, ". . . all things . . . work together for good to those who love God, to those who are called according to His purpose" (8:28), and repeated it several times every day. Soon he began to see positive results of his joblessness. He was able to take areas of concern which his wife had been struggling with alone and be available when his family needed him. He began to think of changing his type of work and pursuing something which would give him more time at home during the crucial years of his children's teens.

Ben was more fortunate than many men who experience a job loss when they're in the forties or fifties. He had placed his confidence in the Lord Jesus Christ and was able to draw upon His strength at a time when he felt defeated as a man.

Stories such as Ben's have no ending. He is in a business now which is giving him greater freedom and less pressure. Having weathered the trauma of the job loss, another crisis in his life will undoubtedly be met with the same faith.

Negative reactions to very real crises during the middle years surround us. We see the man who thinks he is finished and begins to compensate by finding younger female companions. Or the man in the middle years may try to regain confidence by changing his life-style and family style. Statistics on divorce for those who are beyond the young-married stage are revealing. One-fourth of the 1,000,000 couples who divorce annually have been married fifteen years or more. Between 1970 and 1976 there was a 50 percent increase in divorce among couples married twenty years or more (*Kindred Spirit,* Dallas Seminary magazine, Fall, 1977).

It would be presumptuous to assign any generalized statement for the breakup of long-term marriages, but certainly one of them must be the desire on the part of a man for the assurance that he can be attractive and desirable to a younger woman.

A man whose confidence comes from the knowledge of the Lord has the resources to help him put together the shattered pieces of his life or dreams in his forties and fifties. There is a Proverb which says: "For the LORD will be your confidence, And will keep your foot from being caught" (Proverbs 3:26).

What happens when your foot is caught? You're trapped and helpless in the onslaught of the problems coming down the road. We had a perfect illustration of this in our neighborhood. Snuffy is a nearly blind, arthritic old dog who belongs to my neighbor. One day I heard horns honking in the street in front of our house and went outside to see about the commotion. There was Snuffy sitting in the middle of the road, holding up traffic from both directions. He didn't move an inch, in spite of the shouts from the occupants of the cars. I ran into the street to retrieve Snuffy and discovered that he had a toenail caught in his sweater and couldn't budge. I freed him from his trap and he waddled slowly home. Poor old Snuffy was at the mercy of the world while his foot was trapped.

A man's midlife crisis may come in many forms, but physical incapacity is one of the most traumatic. Ron is the principal of an elementary school. Late one night he was riding a bicycle and was struck by a hit-and-run driver. For weeks Ron fluctuated in a vague zone of confusion. When he began to regain a small amount of his mental capacity, it was discovered that he had lost his ability to communicate and that words would come out as scrambled as a crossword puzzle. Each little advance was a major victory, but the doctors did not hold out much chance for recovery of his memory or full mental capacity. He began to slip into an attitude of indifference. The turning point came on the day when his wife, Julie, said, "Ron, you must get well. There are hundreds of people praying for you right now. Stop relying on your own ability to get well and let Christ be your strength."

Ron said later that he could scarcely comprehend what his wife was saying, but enough penetrated his consciousness to make him realize he couldn't give up because God hadn't given up on him.

Today Ron is back at the school, his speech is restored, although a bit hesitant, but his testimony is strong.

Where did Ron's life support come from? His loyal wife and children, certainly, but even their unfailing love was inadequate to bring him out of his brain-damaged stupor into a world of reality.

The answers for the problems of this time of life are to be found in the flavor of vine-ripened fruit. When a person has been a branch growing from the true Vine, who is Jesus Christ, that branch will produce fruit with a flavor which is irresistible. The Bible says, "I am the vine, you are the branches; he who abides in Me, and I in him, he bears much fruit; for apart from Me you can do nothing" (John 15:5).

In this day of green, unripened fruit and vegetables, we are encouraged to buy this type of produce with the promise that "you can just put it on the window sill for a couple of days and it will ripen." Fruit doesn't ripen separated from the branch—it rots!

If someone has a better way to meet the challenges of the middle years, apart from a personal relationship with Jesus Christ, then the fruit must be injected with preservatives and false coloring. It may be flavorful, but it will never supply the world with good nutrition.

A Woman's High Noon

A recent best-seller on the stages we go through in life said of a woman's middle years, "It is imperative that a woman find a sense of importance and a means of independent survival before the empty nest leaves her feeling superfluous" (Gail Sheehy, *Passages*).

For the woman who has been holding down a job and being a homemaker, there are the inevitable concerns about health, stamina, job security. However, for the woman who has not been earning a living independent of her husband's support, one of the first things she begins to think about is going to work.

We visited Sue and Don shortly after she had taken a job in an office. We had known Sue thirty years ago when she was a skilled registered nurse, working a full schedule and earning good wages. Over the years she had four children and had become, as her husband described it, a "Super Mom." When she decided to reenter the job market, she was terrified. She said, "I never felt so insecure and inadequate in my life. I had been a nurse, cook, chauffeur, secretary, teacher, counselor, and general housekeeper for thirty years and suddenly I was told that I wasn't qualified for anything." Sue's story is multiplied many times. A recent study at the Yale University School of Medicine found that "almost 40% of American women looking for a paying job after years of homemaking suffer from depressive symptoms and stress" (*Family Circle,* September 20, 1977).

A woman in her middle years needs what Joan, the brilliant wife of a business executive, called "self-validation." She needs to know she is important to someone, has a useful purpose to fulfill in life. Joan said that when her children were growing up she knew she could not successfully combine raising them with outside work. She had been active in community, social, and political organizations, but gradually began to find herself needing something which would satisfy her desire for more intellectual stimulus. After becoming disenchanted with political overtones in her church, she decided to attend a Bible study and find out what it was all about. She plunged into a large women's group which was studying the minor prophets and thought, "I don't belong here. This doesn't make sense at all." She tried to use her educational background for understanding the basic truths of the Bible and found it inadequate.

Joan had her eyes and heart opened to a personal relationship with Jesus Christ in an unusual way. She went to see the movie "Sound of Music" and heard the Mother Superior tell Maria, "When God closes the door He opens a window." She thought about that for a long time and when she admitted that she could not intellectualize the Bible, but had to accept it on faith, the window was opened to understanding the truth of God.

Joan is using the educational background and her keen mind to pursue a latent talent in writing which she had not sharpened during her homemaking years. She has discovered that self-validation is in knowing the security of the Lord.

The middle years can be fantastic for a woman who knows her worth, who has an excitement for the challenges. God didn't promise us freedom from difficult circumstances—He promised us freedom in Christ. He gave us the ability to be creative, first in the physiological fact that we could bear children, and next in those gifts of creativity which are distinctively a part of the feminine psyche.

The high noon of a woman's life can be a time of great refreshment. For the first time she may be able to think of doing something different, of taking up a new hobby, a new sport, or a new career. When the peanut-butter-and-jelly days start to fade, the gourmet dining may begin.

There are so many opportunities awaiting the woman in her midyears. However, one of the things she could do is plan before the empty-nest syndrome takes its toll. She could read, talk with other women who have found fulfilling pursuits, make lists of things she enjoys, test some directions. A principle the Bible gives us about planning for tomorrow comes from Ephesians 5:15, 16, where it says, "Therefore be careful how you walk, not as unwise [women] but as wise, making the most of your time . . . ."

Marriage in the Middle

It's an accurate commentary on today's society to have people applaud when it is announced that a couple have been married over twenty-five years. That may be an accomplishment in perseverance or an adventure in growth. It's such an important subject today that one of the women's magazines is featuring a series called "Marriages That Work." The writers said, "For most people in a good marriage, the early, middle and late years are all one long period of adjustment and readjustment" (*Family Circle,* September 20, 1977).

When we talk about adjustment and readjustment in marriage, the only one we can adjust or readjust is ourselves. It sometimes takes a few years—or a few decades—for individuals to finally realize that they cannot change their spouse.

I was speaking at a conference one weekend when a woman came to me with a big smile and said, "Carole, I was so glad to hear you say that your husband dropped his clothes on the floor and didn't close the closet door. My husband does the same thing and I want to know what you do about it."

I was prepared with a deep theological answer. I said, "Well, I just pick them up, close the door, and consider what the alternative would be if I didn't have them to pick up or close."

On the other hand, my husband tolerates my aggravating way of interjecting irrelevant topics into a conversation. He may ask a simple question such as, "Did you pick up my suit at the cleaners?" and I'll reply, "That reminds me, did you tell Keith to get his hair cut?"

What can make a midlife marriage sizzle? The same things which added the glow twenty or thirty years before, combined with more experience. Dr. Paul Tournier, the famous Swiss counselor, gave some of his principles for a totally successful marriage. He said first that everything should be shared. He listed these areas of sharing: interests, disappointments, victories, money, worries, work, housekeeping, children, and social and spiritual vocation. He also said that a couple needs to be completely open with one another, what he called an "honest transparency" (*Eternity,* November, 1974).

It's not easy to be transparent with anyone, especially with the one you marry. However, human frailties can make your partner more endearing and tender confessions build a stronger bond.

For many, the phase of middle age and the accompanying challenges is superimposed with another change, which is either another step to fulfillment or another reminder of the intrepid time machine.

"I can't believe it . . . we're going to be grandparents! We're much too young to have grandchildren!"

Phase VI

Third Generation Shock

13

Are Grandparents Necessary?

Dear God:
My grandma says things were different when she was a girl. Were You in charge then, too? I would like to know.

Your friend,
SALLY

Jesus Christ is the same yesterday and today, yes and forever.
Hebrews 13:8

What's so special about grandparents? They're the same people who struggled through the measles and mumps stages—the ones who paced the floors at 2 A.M. when their teenager was out—the couple who struggled with heartache and soared with victory. Grandparents are the same confused humans who thought they were making a mess out of raising their children and suddenly developed tremendous insight on how their grandchildren should be raised.

Being a grandparent is a special gift from God. Being a special grandparent is a vital part of the support system of a family. A grandparent is necessary to build a treasure house of memories. A grandparent is necessary to love without reservation, to give without qualification, to understand without condemnation.

The fortunate ones who have had special grandparents have new dimensions added to their lives.

Dimension: Security

Debbie has special grandparents. She began to talk about them while we were standing outside the church and people started to glance at her

135

sympathetically, because she was soaking the patio with her tears. She loved her grandparents so much that she couldn't talk about them without emitting a flood of emotion.

"My grandma and grandpa are so special because they make me feel so secure. Even if I'm rebelling against my parents—and I have done that— they don't see my bad side. They don't have much money, but they give me so much. I just feel good when I'm with them."

What's so special about grandparents? It's the security they give, the refuge in a world where the other kids make fun, parents make demands, and teachers don't understand.

My grandfather came from Sweden as a young man. His name was Godfrey Johnson, a tall, wiry man with bright blue eyes and a deep chuckle. On the long voyage from the old country, he discovered there were so many Johnsons on the ship that when he arrived in America and approached the immigration authorities, he said his name was Godfrey Carlson. (He thought that would be a more uncommon name.) Consequently, from the time I was a little girl I can remember my grandfather teasing my grandmother about the fact that she had married Godfrey Carlson, whose name was really Johnson, and therefore, she wasn't married at all. My grandmother, a very devout Swedish Lutheran, would always take her starched apron from around her ample waist and pretend to shoo my grandfather with it. This was a very predictable little scene whenever we went to Grandfather's house, and I would always provoke it by asking how my name happened to be Carlson.

The pattern of my visits to Grandfather's was a part of the security of my childhood. Grandfather always held my hand and stroked my hair. His hands were rough from the manual work he did, but I loved to have him tell me that my hair was so soft. Grandmother never touched me or hugged me; it was contrary to her unemotional Scandinavian temperament. However, she loved me in her own special way because she always baked the big round sugar cookies I loved.

Grandma's sugar cookies are extinct today. What a shame. The anemic rounds of dough glued together with a thick layer of gummy sugar icing are poor substitutes for the buttery cookies with the sugar granules clinging to them.

Security has many faces. It may even be the predictability of the stories. Grandfathers and grandmothers, to the despair of their sons and daughters, do repeat the same stories. However, to grandchildren, stories don't grow stale. Anyone who has read the same book to the same children a hundred times knows the truth of that statement.

Grandmother was always disturbed when Grandfather burped. It was never a polite little *humph* behind a napkin, but a loud and resounding **buurrrp** for all the world to hear. He would then look solemnly around the table while the children bit their lips waiting for the inevitable proclamation. "All right," Grandfather would say seriously, "let's bring that up again and we'll vote on it."

Security is also someone to listen when everyone else seems to be so busy. "My grandpa took me for a walk and we talked about lots of things . . . but mostly food and work," Brian, a seven-year-old, said. "What kind of work did you talk about, Brian?" I asked. "Oh, the kind of things people do when they work. I never really understood why people go to an office and what they do there, but Grandpa told me lots of things and said he'd take me to his office." Security is knowing what grownups do when you're in school.

Dimension: Building Memories

In the primary grades the children who were asked about their grandparents all began to tell where they took them. They went to Disneyland and Knott's Berry Farm, to Catalina and to the mountains. To hear the children talk, it would seem that grandparents were spending an extraordinary amount of time just going. But that's what is special about grandparents. They build memories for the time when memories are needed. The sight of a puny little box of blueberries, inviting me to buy them at some outrageous price, reminds me of the time my grandfather took me blueberry hunting in Northern Wisconsin. A rowboat may recall when Grandfather taught the painful experience of patience in fishing. Strawberry ice cream is a reminder of the thick homemade concoction painstakingly turned in the ice-cream freezer at Grandma's house on the Fourth of July.

A beautiful grandmother, the wife of Dr. Louis Evans, noted author and preacher, said that every summer she had her grandsons at their lake home for eight to ten weeks. She said, "We were so close to each other and I wanted the time they spent with us to be something they would always remember." What did Mrs. Evans do to make this a time of building memories? Were they exciting, creative games that we could publish in a book entitled *Strictly for Grandparents?* Not entirely. Mrs. Evans said,

"Oh, mostly I just cooked. The boys played and swam so hard that they were hungry all of the time."

Memories can be built in the kitchen by grandmothers. One of the girls in the high-school class at our church said, "All grandmothers are good cooks." That statement gave me a resolution about my own culinary shortcomings.

Distance or death will separate the generations, so building memories when the material is available is important.

My prayer as a grandmother:

Lord, give me the perception to halt the busyness of my life to capture the wonder of living. Let me hear above the telephone to the "why" in my grandchild's question. Let me halt the unimportant errands to show the "how" to my grandchild's inquiry. Lord, give me the patience with the attention span of a child, but the firmness to establish loving discipline. Above all, Lord, may I never take away the rights of his parents to be parents.

Dimension: Education

Ruth and Billy Graham have fourteen grandchildren, as of the last count. When their own children were small, and Billy was absent from home for periods of time, it was the fact that Ruth's mother and father lived across the street from them that gave their children such a sense of stability. Ruth said that her mother was an "ideal grandmother." "She was always making doll clothes for the girls, and taught them how to sew." Both grandparents read to the children and played games with them.

As the Graham children grew up and had children of their own, they all attributed so much of their love of the Bible to their grandparents. As Ruth became a grandmother herself, she said that one of the most important things for a grandparent to know is that grandchildren are not their responsibility. They are to *enjoy,* never to correct. It's up to the parents to do the discipline, although, of course, Grandma and Grandpa must see to it that the children behave.

The stability which is a factor for one generation can be a continuing line, affecting many generations to come. One of the most tender illustrations of the influence of a grandmother is in the second letter of Paul to Timothy. Timothy was like a son to Paul, and when Paul gave credit for the kind of a young man Timothy was, he said, "I know how much you trust the Lord, just as your mother Eunice and your grandmother Lois do . . ." (2 Timothy 1:5 LB). A godly grandmother was a link in the life of one of God's choice men, young Timothy.

Dimension: Unselfish Love

The Living Bible says "An old man's grandchildren are his crowning glory . . ." (Proverbs 17:6).

There's something so special about being a grandparent. The new dimension added to life says, "There's nothing you can do for me, I just want to love you."

The love of a grandparent for grandchildren doesn't ask for anything, demand anything, or need anything. A little smile, a little hand placed trustingly, is enough reward. The contribution of grandparents to the third generation is one of love shown in many little ways.

One day at the checkout counter of the supermarket I watched a clever four-year-old boy try to wheedle his grandmother out of some candy. She said, "We're going home right now to get something really good for lunch. No candy now, honey." He looked at her with the plan that he had one more ace up the sleeve of his T-shirt and said, "Mommy and Daddy don't care."

Grandma said, "But I care. Now look at this book. Can you tell me about the pictures in here?"

And with the insight that only experience can bring, she began to point out stories in the pictures in a magazine while the checker was ringing up the groceries.

Grandparents are for reminding worried parents about the problems they had growing up. When two-year-old Susie is difficult to toilet train, or fifteen-year-old Mike gets a critical note from his teacher, it's Grandma or Grandpa who can say. "You were the same way, and you turned out okay."

Most grandparents do not have the demands, the constant surveillance, or the daily exhaustion of raising their grandchildren. They can save their energy for the joy of just loving.

Doug, a fifth grader, said, "Grandmas and grandpas are special because they're not around all the time."

Grandparents Don't Need to Be Related

Helen and Gene are grandparents to dozens, perhaps hundreds, of boys and girls, young men and women, but they're not related to them. When they moved into their small suburban home, a little girl and her younger brother came across the street to help and watch. A few days later they came over with a request. "We want to start a club," they said.

Helen laughed and replied, "I don't know anything about the Girl Scouts or the Boy Scouts, but I like to tell Bible stories."

"That's okay, just as long as it's a club."

Helen began the Good News Club and at the first meeting, eleven boys and one girl, in the third through the fifth grades, came. From that small beginning Helen and Gene taught, camped, played, and laughed with many children throughout the years. Some of the results of that little club have been (1) a football player who was first string at the University of Southern California; he went on to be an outstanding coach who has helped shape the lives of many young men; (2) a girl who married a military career man; she later became a staff member of Campus Crusade for Christ. This couple was in one of the original groups on the UCLA campus in which a young man gave his life to Christ and became the minister of one of the outstanding churches in Southern California; and (3) another girl who raised seven children, all of them Christians.

These were just a few of the "children" in the Good News Club who expanded their influence to countless hundreds, perhaps thousands. Helen and Gene are truly special spiritual grandparents.

When You Are One

A dear friend of mine breezed into the house while I was preparing for the visit of my little granddaughter. She said, "I can't for the life of me figure out what's so special about being a grandmother. Doesn't it make you feel old all of a sudden?"

I said, "I didn't think it was anything special, either, until I was one. You can't know what it's like to be one until you are one."

After all, your grandchild thinks you're funny. You never really know whether he thinks you're funny-witty or funny-ridiculous, but it doesn't really matter.

Your grandchild thinks your house is neat to explore, and never notices the dust balls or dirty windows.

Your grandchild demands so much, expects so much, and receives so much of that priceless commodity of love.

It's special to be a grandparent—until you're not so agile anymore. It's special to be a grandparent—until your eyes can't see to sew or read, your ears distort the sound of words, and your legs or hands are plagued with arthritis. Slowly, surely, the special grandparent may become the special problem and then the big question comes: *What do we do with them now?*

Phase VII

Citizens With Seniority

14

What Do We Do With Them Now?

And even when I am old and gray, O God, do not forsake me.
Psalms 71:18

Americans have yet to come up with the answers, but more and more are at least asking themselves the questions that most must face sooner or later: What do we do with our parents?
Time *magazine*
June 2, 1975

When my mother was eighty-eight years old I had to make a decision which threw me into a cloud of guilt. I thought I had killed her. For two months she had been hovering between life and death after an operation which was so severe the doctors were astounded that she survived. She was being sustained by many of the life-giving machines that modern medicine uses to prolong our existence.

With the assurance that she was getting excellent care and there was nothing I could do to help her, I left for the East to fulfill a writing obligation which was to take me to Europe.

The day before I was to leave, some friends were giving us a farewell party when the long-distance phone call came. I turned icy cold as the doctor said, "Carole, the infection has become worse. I'm afraid we can't prolong her life without some extreme measures . . . and I don't believe she has the heroics to endure them."

I thought of her poor little wasted body, weighing no more than eighty pounds, of her screams of pain when tubes were inserted and removed, and said, "I'll call my brothers and see what they say."

The doctor said, "What is your vote?"

For a moment I thought, does one cast a ballot to elect for life or death? But I answered, "Don't use extreme measures."

When I hung up I began to shake uncontrollably and I ran to my room and cried, "Lord, why did I have to make such a decision? Did I do the right thing? Show me some purpose in all this."

Where was my trust in the omnipotence of God? Where was my reliance upon His wisdom? What happened to my belief that "all things work together for good"? Where was that power I received from the verse, "I can do all things through Christ who strengthens me"?

I thought I had played God in making that awful decision, and yet He showed me that even when we think we're running the show ourselves, He still commands center stage.

My mother is now ninety-one years old, living in a nursing home a few miles from us, entertaining the "old people" with her harmonica rendition of "Home, Sweet Home" and singing gospel songs to anyone who has the fortitude to listen.

For most of us in the middle years there comes a time when we have to make any number of decisions about our elderly parents. With each direction we take the realization becomes more acute that someday someone may be making similar decisions for us.

Dilemma of the Sandwich Generation

What happens to those who are caught between aging parents and roaring teenagers? Ellen said, "I'm pulled in so many directions I feel like a piece of taffy. My parents need me on one side, to do things they can't do for themselves. I run them to the doctor, do shopping, take them to church. But somehow I never seem to be on hand when they need me for something special. I really feel guilty when we go away and they have to depend on someone else.

"On the other side, I have teenagers who are a bigger burden every year. Just to keep them in clothes and shoes is an astronomical bill, let alone trying to set aside money for college. My son uses my car and leaves me stuck, and it's usually the very time Mother calls me to come over. And you should see the laundry! I don't understand why kids can't wear clothes more than once."

Ellen bit her lips and said, "I don't mean to gripe, I really love them, I just wish I could live for myself once in a while!"

Ellen may find consolation in knowing that she is representative of a group of middle-class middle-aged who feel the stress of being part of the "sandwich generation."

Older people and teenagers have a lot in common. Both groups are largely unemployed, or have difficulty getting jobs. Many of the elderly and the teens are introspective and become depressed over circumstances. The highest suicide rates are in these two groups.

"It looks to us now that a major concern of middle-aged people is the care of their aging parents," said Dr. Bernice Neugarten, an internationally known University of Chicago specialist on aging. "And children may depend upon their parents longer, too, because their educations often go on longer than they used to" (*Los Angeles Times,* October 19, 1977).

If there really is a problem, we need to take a realistic look at it, and then see if God has provided any guidelines.

Old Is Getting Older

Growing old is something most of us don't think too much about until we notice the beginning saga of the sag in one of our contemporaries. About that time we may decide not to grow old gracefully, but fight it all the way. Billions of dollars each year are spent on cosmetics (we want to look young). Vitamins, food supplements, and exercise are more popular than Grandma's angel-food cake (we want to feel young). At some point in time every human being, whether he admits it or not, is apprehensive about the inevitable deterioration of getting old.

What is old? The students of gerontology have categories which are called "young-old," the fifty-five to seventy-five-year-olds, and the "old-old," which is above seventy-five. This is only for the sake of chronological placement, not personal attitude evaluation. In the latter category there are certainly some "old-olds" who are under fifty-five and some "young-olds" who are more than eighty. However, the researchers in the field of demography, which is the science of births, deaths, and their relation to population growth, chart a trend today which will cause increasing problems for the country and new challenges for most families.

In the early 1900s only very tough or extremely lucky Americans lived to the biblical three score and ten. Emily Dickinson, American poetess, died when she was fifty-six. Jay Gould, a financier who left a before-inflation estate of 80 million, was also fifty-six when he died. The great American composer, George Gershwin, was only thirty-nine.

. . . In 1900 only 3.1 million, or one out of every 25 Americans, were over 65. Now, 21.8 million, or one out of every ten, fall into this category. The reason for the rise is twofold. Modern medicine has cut infant mortality rates and increased the average life expectancy from 47 years in 1900 to 71.3 today. Since 1957, the U.S. birth rate has dropped . . . increasing the ratio of elderly to young people . . ."

Time magazine, June 2, 1975

Modern medicine has done much to change the population structure of the United States in recent years. What does this mean to us or for our future? Simple. We can expect a continuing growth in the numbers of older people who will make up an increased proportion of the total population.

With life expectancy advancing, does this mean that life quality will keep pace? Not necessarily. New problems which have been creeping toward us in the past few years have developed into a trend that some people believe is as severe as racism. This is the appearance of yet another "ism."

Ageism in America

We are in a youth-oriented society. Can you imagine a television commercial for perfume featuring a great-grandmother? What would happen to a woman's magazine if a citizen with seniority appeared on the cover? Advertising is not geared to the elderly; in fact, in many cases, it downgrades them.

Advertising reminds us that we shouldn't go gray, get wrinkles, or gain weight. Aging in the land of perpetual youth is painful, especially if we look our age or (heaven help us) look older than we are. Shouting from the tube and the slick-colored pages are such words as "Look young again!" "Cover the gray." And there's the ad with the lovely gal in her late twenties, scowling faintly out of the page with the caption, "When did you realize that you looked older?"

Is it because we are geared for such a fast pace, and there is something dishonorable about slowing down? A Christian friend, who is studying in the School of Gerontology at the University of Southern California, suggested that what we proudly call the Protestant work ethic, which applauds those who contribute their productive energy to society, has contributed to the lack of respect for the aging, who no longer are the contributors, but the receivers.

It's a paradox that we in America, a so-called Christian society, could learn from Japan and China about aging. In Japan, respect for the elders is shown in many ways. The most common word for the aged is *otoshiyori,* which literally means "the honorable elders."

The Japanese do not segregate their aged and elderly the way we do. "Over 75 percent of all Japanese aged sixty-five or more live with their children in contrast to 25 percent in the United States" (Steven Zarit, *Readings in Aging and Death,* Harper & Row, 1977).

Obviously there are some attitudes of the Japanese which are not feasible to import, but others are very interesting. They have a Respect for the Elderly Day, which is a national holiday. They use the sixty-first birthday as an occasion to honor the elders and express affection for them. On each bus and train there are certain seats designated for the elders. In some cities in Japan there are programs in which elders living alone are visited or called on a daily basis to see if they are all right or need anything.

In America, the segregation of vast numbers of our elderly is due to the mobility of family life and, in many cases, the breakdown of our family structure, which no longer cares for a parent or relative who lives hundreds or thousands of miles away.

One sunny afternoon I was in a local park and watched a microcosm of American thought unfold. The young mothers were watching their children play on the swings and slide, while some of our citizens with seniority were sitting on benches feeding the pigeons. A few children were playing with a Frisbee, which was thrown toward an elderly man in a rumpled suit, who was wearing a gray fedora on that warm day. One little boy ran toward the man to retrieve his toy and you could see the old fellow's face light up. The little boy said, "Hi," with the friendly ease of a child, and his mother sprang into action. "Come back here, Jimmy," she said, pulling her child away quickly. It was an act of segregation of the ages. The smile on the old man's face faded as Jimmy ran to the other side of the playground.

Age is not revered in America; it is feared.

Give Me Value

People who have placed value upon their lives when they were younger need to retain that trait when they are citizens with seniority. We all need to know that we are someone of value.

There are many ways to assure the elderly of their self-worth, and one is to help them stay in their own environment, if possible. Ward's mother has moved three times since her husband died, each time closer to her children. However, when I walk into her living room today, it is exactly the same in furniture placement, color scheme, and appearance, as the living room she shared with her husband. Her location has changed, but the familiar environment has given her security.

So many times after the death of a father or mother, the children, out of concern and love, want the surviving parent to move in with them. Even when a person is no longer able to take care of himself, research has shown in one study that 77 percent of the elderly said that they would choose to live somewhere other than with their children, Zarit reported.

Familiar surroundings, established habits, comfortable patterns should be retained as much as possible. Having some member of the family close, however, is valuable in the later years. One man told me that he and his family attend a church which is more than twenty-five miles from their home. I said, "Why do you go so far to attend church—aren't there any good ones closer to you?"

"Of course," he answered, "but my grandmother lives near the church and we drop in to see her every Sunday. It's the bright spot in her week."

In the rural sections of America that might be a common practice, but it was refreshing to hear an executive in an urban area revive that old-fashioned practice.

Value is in doing something useful. There are people who remain useful until they are completely infirm; there are those who will not know how to be useful when their homemaking or income-producing abilities wane, and there are others for whom we need to invent something useful.

Tom's grandmother was a legend in the family. She lived in a little western Kansas town which existed as a railroad station for the wheat farmers. Her husband died when her youngest child was seven years old, leaving her with five boys and a girl to raise. She came from hardy stock—her grandfather was the twelfth president of the United States, Zachary Taylor, who was popularly known as "Old Rough and Ready." When this plucky Kansas woman was in her middle sixties and so asthmatic that she had to gasp for breath at times, she bought a paneled truck, put a piano on it, and went around giving music lessons, and taking orders for pianos in her own moving studio.

On one occasion Tom's grandmother saw the treacherous funnel clouds known to those who live on the plains of West Kansas as killer tornados, approaching her traveling music salon. She hopped out of the truck and crawled into a large cement pipe which ran through a ditch beside the road, weathering out the storm. When the tornado passed, she climbed back in her truck and made the rounds of all her lessons.

That's a woman who remained useful until she could no longer move!

Advanced age does not mean uselessness. Dr. Louis Evans, one of the outstanding Presbyterian preachers of our time, is lecturing, writing, and leading tours to the Holy Land when he's past eighty. John Wesley preached when he was eighty-six years old. Michelangelo, one of the greatest artists of all times, created beautiful works when he was past eighty. Tennyson was eighty-three when he wrote his famous poem "Crossing the Bar." Grandma Moses was seventy-six before she owned her first paint brush. Corrie ten Boom works on her books and films every day and she's past eighty-five.

God gave us this principle in the Psalms: "Even in old age they will still produce fruit and be vital and green" (Psalms 92:14 LB).

God never intended His children to end their days in meaningless activity.

Sometimes creative children or grandchildren should invent activities to make the older loved one be useful. There's a church in our area whose minister has a daily radio program. He has booklets which he gives to his radio audience upon request and his mailings are staggering. Every morning there are ten or fifteen elderly men and women stuffing envelopes, doing the mailings, and having a marvelous time talking and joking. They are making a contribution and receiving a benefit at the same time.

Give Me Dignity

When your elderly loved one reaches the age and stage when we must practice role reversal, his need is acute to retain his dignity. One of the cruelest tactics of humanity is to strip a man of his sense of personal worth.

Here's a daughter who is gradually placed in the position of being a mother to her mother. How does she reverse her role without degrading her mother? One of the ways may be with questions. "Mother, would you like me to take over writing your checks and balancing your account for you? I could do it easily right along with mine." Role reversals are not done with a leather whip but with a cotton ball—as soft as possible.

Having been a visitor in nursing homes for the past few years, I have observed firsthand the ways to strip a person of his or her dignity. If it becomes necessary to have your elderly loved one in a full-care facility of this type, there are some observances to make and some attitudes to develop.

First of all, does the home have an atmosphere of cheerfulness? Do the attendants smile and speak to the residents with interest? Is it clean and tidy? Are the lights answered soon or do the patients have to wait a long time for attention?

Some people living in nursing homes love them. They feel comfortable with the routine, they like the stimulus of group activities, and they enjoy the security of being cared for. For several years I've stopped and talked with Thea, who has her favorite seat on the end of the couch near the front door. One day the nursing home got a new couch and Thea was very irritated because she had made her impression on the old one and the new couch was too hard. However, after a few days Thea had her blue shawl spread across the back of the sofa and she was contented. I asked her one day if she would like to go for a ride or a walk outside. (She was capable of walking and was not infirm.) She said, "My, no, dear, I might lose my seat on the couch."

Helen hates the nursing home and makes life miserable for her faithful husband, who stays with her every day from two to five. The minute Bill walks in she begins her complaints. One day I discovered this was their way of staying alert in their aging surroundings. Helen had a stroke ten years ago and Bill cared for her faithfully until it became too difficult for him. They have been married almost sixty years, and their pattern has always been that she complains and he makes fun of her.

A person in a nursing home needs his or her own identity. A clock big enough to see, personal gowns instead of the harsh and drab hospital robes, pictures of the family, are all so important.

There's a principle which was given in the Jewish Law which says, "You shall rise up before the grayheaded, and honor the aged . . ." (Leviticus 19:32).

The Touch System

When eyes are dim and ears are dulled, we still may retain our sense of touch. One of the greatest communication tools between all ages is that precious sense of touch.

Try brushing the hair of an elderly woman, or rubbing Grandpa's back. These are acts of love which take no money, little effort, and scarcely any time. But the memory lingers on. Alice, who was blind, was a patient at the nursing home. Whenever I went into her room she would grab my hand and stroke it while she told me about her nine children and forty-four grandchildren. "Forty-four grandchildren! I can't believe it, Alice, you look so young." She'd laugh and slap my hand so hard I would wince. Alice's great joy in life was to touch and be touched.

Whenever a child goes into a home where the elderly live the most important thing is the sense of touch. Skin so young and smooth restores memories and encourages tired bodies.

Myths of the Aging

Advanced age does not necessarily mean a decline in intelligence. One of my mother's many roommates in the nursing home was a woman who had traveled extensively, taught languages in high school, and was a charming conversationalist. A nurse's aide came in with her supper tray and said, "Here's your supper, honey! Now be sure to eat everything like a good girl." The remark was just one indication of the condescending manner some people use toward their elders. In the nursing home the patients are called by their first names, which in many cases I believe is disrespectful. My mother is hard of hearing but sharp of mind, but sometimes she is treated like a dull-witted child.

People of average health can expect to maintain or even increase their level of performance into old age. It was exciting and encouraging to read of an extensive study by some psychologists who said, "In our opinion, general intellectual decline in old age is largely a myth. During the past 10 years, we and our colleagues have worked to obtain a better understanding of intelligence in the aged. We have discovered that the old man's boast, 'I'm just as good as I ever was,' may be true, after all" (Baltes and Schale, *The Myth of the Twilight Years,* Readings, edited by Steven Zarit).

In this age of activism the one group which is going to make its voice louder is that of America's older citizens. They call themselves the Gray Panthers and their leader is a feisty woman, Maggie Kuhn. Ms. Kuhn is seventy-two and has a battle plan, she says, to destroy some of the myths surrounding aging. Here are the myths she wants to demolish: Number one, that *old age is a disease* (she says this is reinforced by the medical establishments and the media.) Number two, that *old age is mindless.* Number three, *old age is sexless* (you would be amazed at the number of studies being done at the USC Gerontology Center on this subject). Number four, that *old age is useless,* and number five, that *old age is powerless.* The Gray Panthers are out to fight discrimination against the aged (*Los Angeles Times,* October 26, 1977).

Beyond Social Action

Old age can be a mellow, beautiful time, for a child of God. However, planning for old age should take place during the earlier phases of our lives. In each realm of our being there is a principle called "use it or lose it." The life of a Christian is not divided into little compartments, separated by brick walls. We are living in a physical realm, operating in a social atmosphere, and encompassed by our spiritual life. The preparation we make in the early part of our lives for every aspect of our existence will pay dividends when we become citizens with seniority.

Not everyone is born with a strong body or good health. When the apostle Paul wrote to Timothy he gave him advice about taking care of himself during his "frequent ailments." Paul himself was afflicted with a constant illness. The Hebrew prophet, Jeremiah, complained, "Why has my pain been perpetual And my wound incurable, refusing to be healed?" (Jeremiah 15:18).

However, even for those who are not blessed with health, God has many promises. One reason for physical ailments is in order that ". . . the works of God might be displayed in him" (John 9:3).

When we are blessed with reasonable good health, the Bible gives us guidelines to use to keep our health into old age. Today there is an increased emphasis upon good nutrition, exercise, and rest. We really have no excuse for not knowing the basic elements of physical health. "My people are destroyed for lack of knowledge . . ." (Hosea 4:6). The time to use that knowledge is early in life, before it's too late.

My own father shunned exercise all of his life. The most vigorous sport he enjoyed was sitting in a rowboat for six or eight hours, fishing for bass or perch. When he was in his fifties he bought some land in the country and decided to be a "gentleman farmer." He hired old Daddy Barkdoll to do the planting and weeding, and every day my father would survey his garden and orchard, proud of his increasing crops. My father suffered one heart attack after another and died in his middle fifties. Old Daddy Barkdoll just went on digging and hoeing until he was ninety.

The first principle of aging is *to use the body God gave us carefully and wisely.* He said it was to be the temple of His Holy Spirit. For everyone concerned about air pollution, water pollution, and land pollution today, the Christian should realize that the greatest pollution is what we do to the house in which God lives, which is our own body.

The second principle of aging is *to use the mind God gave us before disease or illness dulls its edge.* There are so many outlets available today to expand our interests, to enlarge our horizons. An active mind before the aging process begins will have more opportunity to stay sharp in the twilight years. Probably one of the saddest commentaries we could hear from people who are capable of seeing is the remark, "I just don't have the time to read." Eyes capable of seeing a printed page may become incapable of distinguishing print someday. There's a publisher who has a slogan READ FOR YOUR LIFE, and that is a universal truism.

Madame deBlecourt is a delightful Dutch woman in her undisclosed upper years. She escorted me in and out of museums in Holland, describing the artist, his style, and the history of each painting. I never learned so much about the Dutch old masters in such a short time. Madame de-Blecourt, however, had to stand within two inches of a painting before she could discern what it was. She laughed as she almost pressed her nose against a picture and said, "It's certainly fortunate I learned all about these before my eyes went. Now I can see art through your eyes."

Guideline: "And do not be conformed to this world, but be transformed by the renewing of your mind . . ." (Romans 12:2).

Third principle of aging is *to love people and develop friends before our world shrinks around us.* There are lonely, embittered old people who have lived for themselves and their family, without developing any friendships or social outlets in the early years. A woman who is completely wrapped up in her family may find that it is not the security blanket she wants in her old age. The man who lives just for his business may discover that he is empty when the office and telephone are silent.

Everyone is attracted to people who are positive, no matter what the age. The old person who complains that no one cares for him or visits him may have reached that point after years of self, business, or family-centered living.

"A joyful heart is good medicine, But a broken spirit dries up the bones" (Proverbs 17:22).

Use it or lose it. The fourth principle of aging is the most important. A dear old saint who has grown in the Lord is one of the most delightful human beings to know. The story of a lifetime of walking with Jesus Christ is greater than the testimony of all the Christian books on the best-seller list. When we look at a person like that, the fear of growing old is lifted.

When we are young in chronological age there are so many things which want to push God down on the priority list. Bible study? I can do that when I have more time, maybe when I go on vacation. Prayer time? Of course, I pray before every meal. There's plenty of time to spend with the Lord when I'm not so busy.

Building a storehouse of God's treasures in younger years is the best life assurance policy we can buy. The reason is given in the letter to the church at Ephesus:

> I pray that Christ will be more and more at home in your hearts, living within you as you trust in him. May your roots go down deep into the soil of God's marvelous love; and may you be able to feel and understand, as all God's children should, how long, how wide, how deep, and how high his love really is; and to experience this love for yourselves, though it is so great that you will never see the end of it or fully know or understand it. And so at last you will be filled up with God himself.
>
> Ephesians 3:17–19 LB

Hand and Hand With God

As we look at what is the last phase of life, we have to admit that when we are citizens with seniority, it is the sum total of what we have been in all of the other phases. If we have loved ones in this phase, what do we do with them now? If they are not believers in Jesus Christ, the most important thing we can do is to introduce them to the Savior so they can live with Him forever. If they do know Jesus Christ in a personal way, we are His reminders and comforters.

Today there are classes on death and dying; there are courses given on college campuses on the subject. Movies and books are telling us of beyond-and-back experiences. However, the Christian has the only answer. "Therefore we do not lose heart, but though our outer man is decaying, yet our inner man is being renewed day by day" (2 Corinthians 4:16).

Earth has a strong hold on its creatures, which is one of the reasons the glimpses of life after death seem to have such a fascination for most people. It's like New York or San Francisco, "great to visit, but I wouldn't want to live there."

For a Christian, the preparation for beyond is getting ready for the ultimate phase in family life. The Bible says, "Therefore, being always of good courage, and knowing that while we are at home in the body we are absent from the Lord—" (2 Corinthians 5:6).

This is the encouragement we can give to everyone, not just the elderly. However, those who are living on the edge of eternity are closer to the reality of moving from their earthly home to the house which God has prepared.

"For we know that if the earthly tent which is our house is torn down, we have a building from God, a house not made with hands, eternal in the heavens" (2 Corinthians 5:1).

Some of my earthly family have already moved into their heavenly home. Kent is probably flying his airplane through skies with clear visibility, laughing as he performs those perfect lazy eights he never could quite master in the earth's atmosphere. My dad may be sitting in a rowboat on some crystal clear lake, pulling in his limit of bass every day. My father-in-law is probably the president of some ethereal bank with unlimited resources. My sister is waiting to get acquainted with me, because we never really knew each other.

Of all the phases of the family, this is going to be the best. When God established the family in Eden He planned a way for us to live together in eternity. The perfect ending for our beginning.

Come join the family!